# A HUMBLING AWAITING

## LASHANTA DIXON

ISBN: 978-1-7356789-2-4 (Paperback)
ISBN: 978-1-7356789-3-1 (E-book)

Library of Congress Control Number: 2020926032

Title Your Truth Publishing
9103 Woodmore Centre Drive #334
Lanham, MD 20706

www.titleyourtruthpublishing.com

*I dedicate this book to my son, Stefan. You are my blessing and true love. I poured my heart out on these pages to show you that strength, courage, and knowledge can get you far! One day, may you read this book (and many of my others) and find an understanding of yourself through me. I love you!*

*Lastly, I dedicate this book to everyone who may be going through a challenging situation in life! No matter where you are in life, you can come out of it and pull through! You can make it, and you can be successful. You are not your circumstances.*

* * *

# CONTENTS

# INTRODUCTION

Just when I thought I couldn't get any lower than where I already was, here came more trouble, digging a deeper hole for me to bury myself. Taking a quick moment to think of what I should do next made the process seem longer. Would it be best for me to help trouble with this deep hole and start digging it myself? Should I lie in this hole and not fight— turn, walk away, and not face it? Or, should I look trouble in the face and tell it to move along because I'm here to overcome?

I didn't know that I could beat trouble at its own game. Feeling helpless, hopeless, and defeated, I didn't have a second left to waste. "Think! Think quickly!" I said to myself. But nothing— absolutely nothing came to my mind! Here I am— young, gifted, and educated (or so I thought before this storm arose), sitting here without the slightest clue of how to interpret or understand my current situation.

*What is my next move going to be?* I was trapped mentally, emotionally, physically, spiritually, and socially. I was at a standstill in my life, like time had suddenly stopped. *Me— of all people?! Why?* I was the person who had planned goals and an understanding of what I wanted out of life. But that lovable, warm-hearted, free-spirited person I once was started to fade slowly.

Life has its way of sitting you down and making you feel like you have no one, while offering you plenty of trials and tribulations. But it was up to me to stay seated or get up to try again— as many times as needed. So, I pondered. But don't get me wrong, there *was* good in my life. However, because I felt trapped for a long time, it seemed as if my bad outweighed my good.

Things kept happening, and I couldn't see any good in my situation. It had taken a turn for the absolute worst. This cannot be! I've been good to others. A glimpse into my childhood years reminded me of my grandma's wisdom: *Do good unto others as you would like them to do unto you.* But now, I wonder if that saying is a thing of the past. Society is different now. However, I couldn't allow societal influences to alter the wisdom of my upbringing.

Back in the day, I didn't understand the meaning of such wisdom; however, I started to gain insight into its meaning, as I grew older. And as an attempt to understand where the disconnect took place, I reflected on my past. *Where did I go wrong? Have I done good to others?* Over and over, that same question kept playing in my head— *have I done good to others?* And although I'm far from an angel, I was able to answer the question with certainty. *Yes! Of course, I've done good to others.* And even though I made mistakes, I had a good heart in the process.

Now, don't judge me because I answered my own question. I'm just telling you how it is! And since I'm an external processor, I often think out loud. It's something I frequently do. And I've accepted that there is nothing wrong with that! There is so much power in our voice. And sometimes, you just have to speak life over yourself! The only problem is when you engage in conversation with yourself. Of course, that would be weird— *right?*

*But anyway, back to my point...*

My mind was scrambled, but still racing like the speed of light. For the most part, I thought I did good to most people, especially my family and friends that I loved dearly. *But did that count for anything? Aren't I supposed to show love to all people?* "But that's impossible," I thought. To be honest, there have been times when I didn't care much for others. I was so quick to get back at someone who disrespected or harmed me. I often leaped at every opportunity to express how I felt or give my opinion because I felt the need to.

Being shy, as a young girl, did not help at all. Allowing others to make me feel like less of a person destroyed my confidence, but ultimately influenced my outspoken, careless nature as I grew older. As time went on, I decided that I would not allow anyone to make me feel that way again; therefore, I often expressed how I felt and didn't care how it was interpreted or perceived! *No sweat off my back!* Well, that's what I thought until life matured me.

I swore to never silence myself again. So, I just told it how it was—or rather— how I saw it. So, maybe I began digging this hole at a young age, being misunderstood and misguided, while unknowingly placing my future in desperate need. *But— wait a minute!* I've been good to others. *Doesn't that count? Wasn't that good enough?* Or maybe, I was just as 'good' as I defined good to be. Maybe my definition of good may not actually be good enough. So, as a result, I sat still, contemplating and comparing all of the good versus the bad things I'd done throughout my life.

After countless hours, I came up with a few things based on what I could remember. "Here goes nothing," I thought. My good outweighed my bad, but not by much. And as I tried to think of other good things I'd done for others, it hit me. Although my good actions outnumbered my bad ones, the magnitude and weight of those bad things seemed to outshine the good. And in terms of physics, negative energy can never be destroyed; it can only transfer. So, based on the numbers, I did more good than bad. However, if I factored in the impact, harm, and damage I caused with my bad actions, then I began digging this hole a long time ago. Therefore, I haven't done more good than bad. And facing that truth was shocking!

I can't believe this! *What have I done? Have I allowed myself to become someone I never wanted to be?* Yes, I did! Thinking back, it stared when I swore to myself that I wouldn't allow another person to hurt me and get away with it. That irrational way of thinking brought out the worst in me. And now, I have to correct this— *but how?* When I said that I would never allow anyone to harm me again, it influenced my thinking, behavior, and reactions. But I didn't recognize this until afterward.

When someone harms you, it's easy to fall victim to a negative mentality. Based on that mindset, I allowed others to influence my behavior. If someone gave me negativity, harm, or disrespect, I gave it right back. It was as if I reflected their actions right back onto them. I put so much out, and now I wonder how I can take all of this back! There's no way! What's done is done! However, negativity can be offset with love! Therefore, I can always respond with love, even when someone else is being negative. For every negative action, a positive reaction can counteract it. *And perhaps, this may create balance? Maybe!* So, I considered a different approach. Mathematically speaking, two negatives equal a positive. But in life, two negatives create more negativity that can do more damage than good!

For many years, I was surrounded by negativity that infested my thoughts. Not knowing what to do, I paced across my living room floor, replaying the things I've done in my head. And like a record player that had a scratch, one thought kept coming to mind— treat others how you would like to be treated. *But wait— shouldn't that standard apply to everyone?* And, if so, it's fair to assume that when someone treats me with disrespect, that that's how they would like to be treated. Right?! Or, once again, maybe I was thinking too deep into it.

With my mind flustered, I continued to pace the floor. It felt like I was in between God and the enemy. It was as if God was sitting on my right shoulder trying to get me to do the right thing, while the enemy was on my left shoulder, trying to redirect my focus on negativity. I was stuck with nowhere to go— in the middle of good and evil. I had to tread carefully because one wrong move could highly impact my life forever.

Feeling like I had a multiple personality disorder, I kept speaking out loud. "Treat others how you would like to be treated, so no... no... no... I cannot continue to think negatively," is what I rehearsed out loud to myself. That immature girl who was shy and afraid to say how she felt came to life in me. *It's just not fair to have to be so nice to people who do me wrong! Why should I have to?* "Lead by example," a voice said. My mature side answered softly, "It's not for them; it's for your own growth." Okay— I think I understand. Now, it's starting to make sense! But at first, my initial thought was to sit in this hole and allow myself to be buried. *Why even bother dealing with this?* For so long, my behaviors dug a deep hole, and now was the time for me to face it. It was time to face the facts and allow my life to disintegrate, so that God could rebuild me into a magnificent masterpiece!

*A masterpiece? Could I actually be a masterpiece?* Or should I say, *can I be rebuilt— piece by piece— to become a positive thinking person?* I know I'll never be perfect because being human comes with imperfections. However, I could improve, and that's what I planned on doing. Meanwhile, I was mentally trapped, trying to unravel my thoughts. So, I laid in this deep hole, reminiscing about my past, holding onto the present, while trying to figure out my future.

Lying there, I decided to cover myself with dirt, starting from the bottom and working my way up. Soiled in the dirt, I felt how it started to break down the essence of my soul. The toxins quickly took over my body like a venomous bite. Every perspective in my life was somehow presented to me. I laid there in the darkness, face-to-face with all of the ugly truths, manipulative lies, and demons that surrounded my environment.

With so many pieces surrounding me, I wondered: *Do I pick them all up at once, or do I omit some? Which pieces go together?* Confused about what to do, I figured I should gather them all, place them in a basket, and work it out from there.

But more negativity crept in. "This won't work," I thought to myself. I allowed those things to consume my mind, affect my health, and take over my soul. Rapidly, I became paralyzed— with nowhere to move or go! It was time to face the inevitable, confront my fears, and tackle my anxiety to prepare for my *beautyfull* comeback. *That's right!* I was ready to be full of beauty!

Lying still in this deep hole, with my eyes closed tight and my body extended long, I was suddenly back in my past. Seeing a vision of my family sitting at the table socializing, while having a joyful time with one another, brought tears of happiness to my eyes. Things hadn't been like this in years! In the vision, I walked around the table and observed how everyone smiled and enjoyed one another. I wondered where things went wrong. My family went through a lot, but it wasn't always like this. I've always wondered how we arrived to where we are now. My mind flicked through clips of my past, presenting the good times I had as a child. It stopped at a moment in my childhood where I felt lonely, afraid, and unappreciated. Still lying in this deep hole, I reviewed my childhood from a different perspective.

When I opened my eyes and got out of that hole, I knew exactly what I needed to do. All of the things I wanted to say to my mother were finally able to come to light. Therefore, I wrote until I could not write anymore. My mind raced with thoughts. *How can I say this without hurting her?* And not knowing where to start, I gravitated toward this thought: *Just tell your story and get it out! Who or what can it possibly hurt?*

Flipping through pages, while flicking my pen, I was so nervous about getting started, but I needed to get it out. So, I got it out. I allowed the little girl inside of me to speak.

*Here goes nothing...*

## ENTRAPMENT

*M*om, *please listen!* All I ask is that you listen. Be open to what I'm about to say to you. Don't judge me. Just listen! You have two ears and one mouth for a reason. It's better to listen than to speak. And I'm sorry, but I really don't want any feedback or advice. *Just listen!*

Now, you may not like what I have to say, but I hope you understand. So, please— *just listen!*

*  *  *

*From day one, when you found out that you were having a girl, I know your excitement went through the roof! You were probably thinking: What will I name her? Will she look like her dad or replicate her beautiful mother? I know you couldn't wait to do my hair, dress me up, and show me off to family and friends! I know that it was an exciting time for you. I was your brand new baby. And despite knowing how much you loved me, I know that mistakes were inevitable.*

> *Now, please hear me; I'm not blaming you for any of the past*
> *decisions or mistakes you made. I know you were young*
> *and were doing your very best. You were a sixteen-year-*
> *old mom with a mom who liked to drink and gamble.*
> *Please listen— I'm not here to judge. I just want you to see*
> *the reality of the situation and understand my perspective*
> *surrounding the life you brought me into.*

> *Your relationship with my dad was rocky. I hardly ever saw*
> *him. And when I did, you two couldn't get along. All you*
> *did was argue, fight, and call each other names!*

She attempted to cut in and respond, but I cut her off. I wanted her to understand that I needed to tell my side of the story without interruption. I wasn't trying to blame her. I just wanted to enlighten her.

> *Mom, please don't stop me from speaking. Please— just listen!*
> *This painful cycle went on for another year. You put all of*
> *your energy into working and trying to keep a roof over*
> *our heads, which I'm grateful for, but it took time away*
> *from me— your daughter.*

> *When I got a little older, you told me that grandma put us out*
> *in the snow when I was a baby. Do you know what*
> *hearing that did to me and how that made me feel? I felt*
> *like I wasn't wanted. And those internal wounds followed*
> *me throughout my entire life.*

> *One year after I was born, another baby came home! It was a*
> *baby by the same man that harmed you— my dad! And*
> *from observing your patterns, I quickly learned that it was*
> *okay to love and have sex with a man who mistreated you.*

> *Mom! Hold on! Please— just listen! I know you have*
> *something to say, but you communicated for so long, and I*

*listened. When you were mistreated, I watched. When you reacted, I learned. Now, for once– it's my turn to talk! So, mom, please listen!*

*When you gave birth to your second child, it took more of your time away from me. We lost so much time that could've been used for us to grow closer together. Otherwise, it was cool having a sibling— especially a brother. I thought, "Maybe he can protect me?" And I grew to see that he did protect me for the most part. Thank you for giving me a little brother.*

*But then, time moved quickly. And the next thing I knew, you were on child number three, without even consulting me! And as a result, even more of your time was taken away from me. The more children you piled on, the more distant we became. I never really got the chance to know you. And at that time, you had dad and three children. But nothing else changed, as you and dad were still fighting and not getting along. It made life very hard for me, as I had to protect my younger siblings, who were at the age of three and four. I didn't know what to do or how to feel. I was just a child, myself.*

*But even more time was lost. I truly wished there was time for me to have fun as a kid and be with you, Mom, but I knew that I had to protect my siblings. Little did I know, that would always be the case in my life  And I often wondered, when will this ever end? This started a trend that continued throughout my life, as the cycle of pain and instability continued.*

*Life, as a child, was certainly not easy. There were many times when the lights were cut off. You would tell me to get candles. It was always "do this" or "do that!" We*

experienced evictions where we found ourselves starting
over. I had to go grocery shopping on my own for the entire
family because you were working. Embracing this life
turned me into an adult way before my time. As I think
back to one sunny day, a lady at the grocery store
questioned me about my age. She could see that I was
young and informed me that I needed someone older to be
with me in the store.

These adult-like responsibilities made me feel like I missed out
on much of my social life and childhood activities. But
never once will I blame you because you had to do what
you had to do. Dad was gone— out doing him! But please,
don't get me started on that topic. Mom— this talk is
for you.

I watched you work hard. You often had two or three jobs at a
time! I know you were tired, but you did what you had to
do for us while we stayed at grandma's house when you
were working. From observing you, I learned that hard
work and determination would get me far, and I owe that
acknowledgement to you. However, at the time, I couldn't
help but see it as more of your time taken away from me!
Some days, you were too tired to go over homework with
me. And some nights, you were too busy catering to my
younger siblings. And for several years, I watched you
work hard, as we moved from one place to another.

Eventually, I thought that I would have some of your time.
But boy, was I wrong! Another man came into the picture.
He took the time that was for me.

A couple years later, another baby was on the way! It was
another person I had to watch over and help. No problem,
Mom! I will do it! I will take care of your new baby, too!

*But despite my willingness, it bothered me that you didn't think to ask me how I felt inside. You just kept piling more and more on my plate.*

*About a year after your fifth child was born, here came another pregnancy! But this time, you came home with two babies. I thought to myself, "What just happened? Did she purchase another child?" Wait a minute, Mom, I am only six! How can I watch seven children?*

*Noticing the hurt, the pain in your eyes, and the weakness that took over your body was painful for me. Observing how this new man took power over you influenced my everyday life. I was subjected to witnessing more violence. Yet again, here was another man who I watched beat, scorn, use, and abuse you.*

*Mom! Wait! Please don't get upset. Please listen. Just let me explain. I didn't know any better at this age, and I didn't realize that this would drastically change my life. I will get to that a little later on. But for now, I need to explain to you how I viewed my childhood.*

*Things were so confusing. One day, I saw how the new man kissed you and held your hand. The next moment, I saw him beating you with those same loving hands. How can love bruise you, leave marks, and then attempt to caress those same wounds? Is this the way of the world? Should I accept this, also? Is this an expectation of all men? Should I not feel loved if he hasn't put his hands on me or hasn't verbally, psychologically, spiritually, and emotionally abused me? Based on my six-year-old perspective, I thought I should hold onto love even though it abused, endangered, and almost killed me. It only made sense, right? Isn't love what we need? Of course! So we should fight to keep it, by any means necessary! And that's exactly what I thought because that's what I saw! Accepting abuse — over and over again— was the story of your life that later influenced the decisions I made in a significant way!*

*But Mom, I have to ask: Did you love him more than you loved yourself? Maybe you didn't have a good understanding of love. Is that why you stayed? What was it? Did grandma not teach you that it's not okay for a man to abuse you? Was your dad present in your life? When I think about it, I never met him.*

*I know you believe that you hid a lot from us. But I have to inform you that you didn't! Maybe you were doing that because you wanted to keep your family together, no matter the circumstances. However, that is not togetherness when we noticed the pain you endured and how afraid you were to speak or say certain things around the man you were with.*

*But it wasn't just him; multiple men abused you. And it hurt that I couldn't help you. All I could do was sit on the side and watch them abuse you, while looking in the face of my siblings, consoling their tears, not knowing how to answer any of their questions. Never once was I asked how I felt. And because my mind often raced with thoughts, it made it hard for me to sleep at night. There was nothing I could do. I felt lost.*

*There was one moment that I will never forget. It was so painful to watch a man drag you across the floor, beat you, humiliate you, speak foul to you, and degrade your existence. He made you undress and beat you while you cried for him to stop. But that man— wait! He cannot possibly be called a man— not after what he did to you!*

*This disgusting, ignorant, horrible coward beat you and threatened to throw you out of the front door into the street with no clothes on! But afterward, you still stayed. What about your self-pride and your self-dignity? Why would you allow someone to treat you like that?*

*I hate that all of this happened to you. I know that it made you angry. I just don't understand why you took your anger out on your children. You may not have known that you did this to us, but we experienced a lot of your anger due to what you went through.*

*Back then, trying to figure out a way to communicate with you was tough. Asking you question after question irritated you. I saw all of the emotions on your face. Your famous phrases were, "I'm okay, so stop asking me so many questions." But the big one was, "We just had a little argument; everything is fine!" What! That's crazy! A little argument?! How can a little argument lead to a big bruise, humongous black eyes, and internal scars that still haven't healed? I knew you weren't okay! Why couldn't you just tell me how you felt and inform me not to allow anyone to ever treat me that way? I really would've loved to talk to you more. Getting insight into your thoughts and feelings probably would have helped me as I grew older. But communication was not your thing!*

*One day, in particular, I found a baby picture, and I asked who that child was. You quickly took the picture out of my hand and didn't respond. I wondered about the child in that picture for so long. I knew that the baby in that picture didn't look familiar at all. The baby didn't look like any of my siblings. And although the child's facial structure resembled ours, I knew that it wasn't any of us. Therefore, I interrogated you until you told me that he was your other child. "Your other child!?" I asked. I know I overwhelmed you with so many questions at once. Where is he? What's his name? Did he die? But all you said was no. No? No, what? You told me that he wasn't dead, but you don't know his name or where he is. You responded, "I gave him up for adoption." I had no idea what adoption was. Adoption? "Someone else has him," you replied. I responded, "Why is it that someone else has him while all of your other children are here?" There was no response. Instead, you looked away, and I noticed that I hit a nerve, trying to quickly dismiss what was obviously painful.*

*Sometimes, I noticed you hiding in your room or the bathroom crying. You thought I was asleep, but I was not. I felt all of your pain. And I prayed that you would someday talk to me; however, you didn't. Maybe it went back to your upbringing. Perhaps you witnessed the same things? Or, maybe, this was our family tradition? But family traditions are supposed to be fun and bring us closer together. But this didn't bring us any closer in a positive way! It only caused pain on top of more pain. It made you even less of a good listener and not an effective communicator. And experiencing that trauma scarred me for life!*

*As time proceeded, I observed the dynamics of our family. I could see how grandma had problems with communicating, as well. How could this be? No one seemed to want to talk or listen. But you all loved to tell us what to do! "Stay out of grown folks' business," was what you'd both say. What about including us in grown folks' business so that we could've had greater insight into life? Including us, by asking how we felt about what was going on around us and how it influenced us, would've been a great start. You forgot to inform us of how to love and be loved! We needed to know about true love. Again, I'm not blaming you— things just seemed to happen the way they did. I guess it was like a domino effect, as this was passed down throughout generations of our family.*

* * *

So much took place, but there was so much more that needed to be released. But in that moment, my mind suddenly went blank. I didn't know what else to say. There were so many instances and experiences that I needed to let go of— that needed to come out. A creepy voice whispered, "Find a way to get it out." Suddenly afterward, another voice said, "To have true peace, pick up those pieces, one by one, and tackle them with strong determination and faith." And because that voice was much more pleasant, I decided to continue the journey that I was called to fulfill. "Thanks," I said, as I postured my mind to continue.

*Now... where did I leave off?*

# 2

# LIFE HAPPENS

Over time, I grew up with mixed feelings toward my mom. I loved her, but I was frustrated by the challenging situations I was placed in. And despite my frustrations with the choices she made, I didn't realize just how much of her ways I adopted as my own. When I got to High School, I started to demonstrate some of the negative behavioral patterns that I witnessed within her previous relationships. I wasn't aware of how much I picked up from her until I began dating.

In High School, I was so in love with a guy named Devin. Not only was he tall and handsome, but he had a car and a job. And I was completely mesmerized by his voice! It was as if he had me under a spell.

During that time, I had friends, but I wasn't on the popular board of directors— *if you know what I mean!* I always saw him hanging out with his many friends during lunchtime. But then one day, he walked over and actually spoke to me!

"Hey, how are you?" he asked. "Fine," I replied, feeling completely overwhelmed with excitement! I could not believe he was actually speaking to me! He went on to ask me my name and my classification. I smiled and replied, "I am a sophomore." I was so eager to answer his question that I forgot to give my name. "And your name?"

he said. "Oh! Yes, my name is LaShanta." "Well— hi LaShanta, I am Devin. You have a pretty smile," he added. After hearing those words, I just about lost it. I was literally jumping up and down in my mind, but I had to keep my composure. No one has ever really complimented me like that— *especially not my smile!* My smile was the one flaw I didn't like about myself, so for him to say that made me feel perfect. It made me feel like he was the one for me! His words gave me such a boost of confidence! But little did I know, Devin would change my life forever.

A few moments later, he asked me for my number and wanted to know if we could hang out and chill. Just hearing those words made me *so* happy! Back then, chill had a completely different meaning. But later on, I soon found that out.

Devin was a senior, so he sometimes left school earlier than other students. I just assumed he left when he was finished with his courses. I was so intrigued, that I noticed every little thing about him. I was still shocked that he asked me for my number. This was surreal. I had so much excitement, that I often sat by the phone and checked it hundreds of times a day, desperately waiting for Devin's call. And after a few days went by, the phone rang. Devin finally called me.

* * *

*Me*: Hello!
*Devin*: Hello! Can I speak with LaShanta?
*Me*: This is she.
*Devin*: What's up with you? How have you been doing?
*Me*: I'm good. I'm just watching T.V. [*Yeah, right!*]
*Devin*: That's what's up! So, when can I see you again?
*Me*: I don't know… maybe this weekend, if you're not busy?!
*Devin*: That sounds like a plan. I will let you know the details.

* * *

I was so surprised that he called me the next day with the date and time that he wanted to come pick me up. He was always the type to take initiative and make me feel special.

On our first date, he tried to woo me and completely melted my heart with a rose. I was in shock. He seemed absolutely perfect. Devin was such a nice gentleman and took me out on multiple dates. We went bowling and to the movies, often, but I was naive to what was really going on.

One day, Devin asked me, "Have you been with anyone else?" I replied, "No, I haven't!" "And you?" I asked. He stated, "Yes, I have!" And based on his response, I knew that meant one of two things: either he's dated other girls or had sex with them. Although I didn't know which, I left it alone.

A few months passed, and I continued to love life and every inch of him. But I could not see what was happening right in front of my face. He had a plan up his sleeve all along!

One day, he invited me to his home. I found out that he lived with his mother and that the car he drove to school was hers. When we entered his room, we watched T.V. But after a while, he moved closer to me. The next thing I knew, he was in my face trying to kiss me.

"No!" I said. "What's wrong?" he said. "Nothing, I just don't kiss," I stated. "Why not?" he inquired. I quickly stated, "Because I don't know where your lips have been!" He laughed, "Girl my lips haven't been anywhere." "Yeah, okay!" I said, sarcastically. But to be honest, I didn't know how to kiss and I surely wasn't going to tell him that. Even still, I didn't know where his mouth had been, so I didn't want to kiss him anyway.

After that awkward interaction, the situation got worse. He leaned over to fondle me and I pushed him away. It was so uncomfortable to be touched in that manner. Without asking me, he kept touching me. "Look," I said sternly, "This is making me feel uncomfortable." "You shouldn't feel uncomfortable— come here..." he stated. He took my hand and tried to place it down his pants. I was so shocked, but because I loved him, I didn't say anything.

Then, he went on to take his pants off and pulled his genitals out.

"Wait a minute! I have not been with anyone— ever! No sex, no nothing!" I boldly stated. "Well, we can take our time," he responded. "Have you ever given oral?" he asked. In shock, I said "Huh?! What's that?" I really didn't know what he was talking about. "Girl— you green!" he said. "Okay, so what does that mean?" I said. He went on to say, "I will explain that to you later. Let's just watch a movie and I will show you what I mean," he said. "Okay!" I said.

So, Devin turned on a sex video and told me to watch it so that I could learn how to *please him*, although the term he used was much more vulgar. "I'm not doing that!" I told him. "Why not?" he inquired. "That's nasty!" I responded. "No, it isn't" he went on to say. But after not giving him what he wanted, he took me home.

Days went by and I didn't receive any phone calls or contact from Devin. I was hurt and did not know what to do. *Should I call?* The voice in my head said not to, however, my heart said to call. So, I finally called, but there was no answer.

Days later, the phone rang. Devin finally called and asked to see me. He set up a time and we met up.

When I arrived at his mother's house, he was there with another guy and two girls who were walking down the steps. I was visibly upset, but he assured me that the guy was his cousin and that the two girls were their homegirls from school. He told me that they were just smoking and chilling. I thought to myself, "Is this the same *chilling* you told me we were going to do the other night, that turned into you putting sex tapes on, while trying to convince me to give you oral sex?"

While we were alone, I couldn't help but ask for details about these 'homegirls' of theirs. "They are just friends. Why are you still asking me about them?" he said, as if he was irritated by my persistence. And since it was clear that he was obviously bothered, due to his tone of voice changing, I decided not to say anything else. He was interested in pursuing another conversation.

And after so many times of trying to convince me to have sex with him, I gave in. I finally did it. Despite knowing that I was not ready to give myself to him in that way, I figured I would do it so that

I could keep him. I didn't know it at the time, but that was such a bad move!

Things went well for several months— until all of a sudden, things changed. He stopped answering my calls and seemed to always be busy. I didn't get to see him as much as I'd like. But thankfully, we were able to arrange a movie night.

I was so elated to see him, that I was ready early. When we finally met up, he seemed irritated, as if he didn't want to be around me. I asked, "What's wrong?" "Nothing," he replied. But before I could get the words out of my mouth to ask again, he told me to shut up. I was shocked and utterly embarrassed. *Why would he suddenly start speaking to me like that? What did I do?*

Over time, I endured more verbal abuse. But at the time, I didn't see it as such because I was so enthralled by him. I just went with the flow and did what I could to keep my man.

Later on, when it was prom season, I asked him to accompany me to my junior prom. He accepted! I was so happy about that! We rented a limo and he came to my house to pick me up in it. It was really nice to have one back then. We took so many pictures and the night started off well. But little did I know, the night would end terribly.

Devin was so controlling. He didn't want me speaking to any male classmates. And when he became aggressive, I walked away and went outside. He followed me outside and grabbed my arm, yelling at me to never walk away from him again! At that point, I was over it, and was ready to go home. So, we left!

After I arrived back home, I took a bath. While in the tub, I realized that I had a bruise on my right arm. But I brushed that off, along with his other acts of verbal and physical abuse. All of the apologies and the "I will never do it again" stories became old— so old, that I couldn't keep up with all them.

I had to make a change. So, I finally worked up the nerve to leave. It wasn't easy, but I knew it was for the best. The hardest part was trying not to remember all of the abuse I encountered in my relationship with him.

So, I picked up my pen and decided to write! But this time, my letter was addressed to my abuser. I'm not sure if he ever read it, but I needed to let it all out. This letter wasn't about him, anyways; it was about me letting it all out so that I could have the freedom I needed.

* * *

*Do you remember...*

> *Remember when I caught you with a female in your house and you told me she was a family member? You told me to wait outside in the rain until she left! I was livid, but I waited.*

> *Remember when you slapped me so hard that I could barely hear out of my ear? Well, I still have that mark on my right ear from the cut that occurred after you hit me!*

> *Remember when I broke up with you over the phone because I was too scared to approach you face-to-face? And you said to me, "I don't care. I only stayed around to have sex with you and to take your virginity, while having sex with other females." I was so embarrassed and wanted to die.*

> *Remember the night that you beat the crap out of me and left me alone without help? I had to figure out how to get to the hospital on my own, and I lied to the doctors and nurses about what really happened to me.*

> *Remember impregnating me and wishing death on me and our unborn child? After I lost my baby, I had low self-esteem because you made me feel like less of a woman. All I wanted to do was die. And where were you? You were out with other women.*

> *Remember coming to my High School cap and gown fitting during my senior year, and dragging me out of the car*

*because I didn't want to do something you wanted me to
do? You left me and you took my cap and gown. I was close
to graduating, and all I wanted to do was die at that very
moment! How could you?*

*Remember coming to my mother's house and banging down
her door after I had to get a restraining order against you
for almost beating me to death? I've never been a snitch or
a "call the police type of chick," but you were out to hurt
me and I had to protect myself. Why did you do this to me?*

*Everything I experienced with you really messed me up! How
could you say that you loved me and beat me the way that
you did? I had many therapy sessions after my abusive
relationship with you. And although it hurt me to my core,
I had to pick up the pieces and move on.*

*And now that I'm gone, I wish you all the best.*

* * *

After writing this letter. I was finished. I had moved on and left him for good. The only problem was that I wound up repeating the same negative cycle— from one bad relationship to the next.

In my next relationship, I found myself feeling lost and afraid. Rodney put a gun to my head and told me that if I ever left him that he would kill me. *How was I supposed to stay and allow him to keep putting his hands on me?* But after seeing that gun, I decided to figure another way out. So, I prayed and prayed. But I swear, it seemed like God just didn't hear me— for years! So, I stayed with him. I didn't have any other options.

One day, I was with Rodney and multiple people who I thought of as family. And then the next thing I knew, I woke up in the hospital with no one by my side. The doctor walked over to explain to me that a rape kit was being done on me because I was found drugged and passed out outside of the hospital. *What?! How could this be?* I was with my boyfriend and close friends. I couldn't remember exactly who it was, but someone was passing around drinks. And my boyfriend was right there! *So, why didn't he protect me?*

As a result of what took place, I stayed away from people for years and disassociated myself from many. People who knew me asked why I was no longer as social as I used to be. But after while, I just ignored their questions.

Many years later, I ran into Rodney and one of his homeboys. He was with one of the guys who were there that night when I was found drugged! I instantly had an anxiety attack just from seeing them both. I couldn't believe it. Rodney had the audacity to actually speak to me and ask me how I was doing. He had some nerve! The voice in my head told me to ask him about that night, but I didn't want to hear anymore lies. And because of that situation, I vowed to never drink with any males, even if we were close. In my mind, males couldn't be trusted. And Rodney was no different.

Rodney was an up-and-coming rapper and was always around females. He would leave for a couple days when he was supposed to be in the studio. So, naturally, I questioned him about other females and their involvement because I didn't trust him. He always got upset when I asked about other females, but I knew he was having sex with them.

When I inquired further, one day, he pushed me down the steps, and the fall broke my arm. Because of this, I was out of work for several weeks. The sorries and the lies were like an old broken record player. I knew I had to go, but making my way out could cost me my life. So, I decided to plan an escape. I decided to file a restraining order and quickly leave when he wasn't home. And although it took a while for me to finally get the courage to leave Rodney, I got out of that relationship with my life and my sanity, although I still felt damaged.

After more therapy and learning to transform my mind from thinking negatively, I got back into the dating scene. I often thought that love must not love me. I was always the hopeless romantic—

wishing to have real love, someday. And one day, I thought that dream finally came true.

One evening, I met an older guy at a club. His name was Gary. He stayed to himself and seemed pretty chill. After conversing, I learned that he had a nice job, no children, and spent his free time volunteering with youth. One thing that he failed to mention was that he'd been incarcerated for fifteen years for murder. I found out that information months later. I tried not to judge him, so I just casually asked him about his past, while we were conversing one day. He was honest with me and told me his truth. Gary stated that it was a "wrong place at the wrong time" situation that took place.

Gary and I continued to spend time together. Everything seemed to be going well. When we met, I wasn't a smoker. But being around Gary, he taught me how to roll backwood and I quickly caught on. And since I mastered it, he always got me to do it.

Life with Gary seemed promising. We enjoyed each other's company and always had a good time. Things were going well, until he decided to have sex with another woman as the result of a bet. In that moment, I was shocked. I couldn't believe this craziness was happening again— especially because of a bet!

I was too tired of foolishness. But then again, I realized that this probably happened because he'd been incarcerated most of his life. So now that he was a free man, he lived life as if he was a young boy without restrictions. But despite my understanding of this, I was furious. Even though he was honest about what took place, his casual response made me even more upset. I trusted him and couldn't believe what he did! And as a result, I couldn't stomach looking at him. So, it was time for me to move on with my life.

Little did I know, Gary continued to contact me, regardless of me changing my number. For years, he continued to call me from several unrecognizable numbers and found me on social media. But since I was never the social media type, I just deleted my accounts. I never found out who gave him my personal information or how he was able to get it!

On multiple occasions, I nicely to asked him to leave me alone, but he just wouldn't listen. He left me messages saying that he planned to take me and start a new life. That only made him sound even crazier! *What type of crap is that? Kidnap me? Really?!* I wanted to call the police, but I was too afraid. Somehow, I felt like he wouldn't do it and was just upset because I left him. Maybe it was his way of crying for help. I don't know, but it wasn't my job to figure it out. So, I moved on.

After dealing with so many cowards, I finally thought that I found the right person for me. I thought that Joe was different from everyone else. That was, until I noticed that he didn't want anything out of life but to sell drugs and stay close to his child's mother. So, I figured, *why should I stay?* And as a result, I was ready to end things. But time and time again, he begged me to stay, every time I planned on leaving. I had this gut feeling that Joe was lying to me, but deep down inside, I wanted to believe him.

"You can't make decisions based upon your past," one voice said. Another voice said, "But you can, and you should know the signs that he is not right." So, I listened to the voice of reason and decided to have a talk with Joe.

It was a brutally honest conversation that we both needed to have. We both recognized and accepted that he still had feelings for his child's mother. But that only made me angrier! *How could someone drag me along for four years, only wasting my time, while talking about me behind my back, discrediting who I am?* I accepted so much foolishness that I declined his offer for us to give things a try. Absolutely not! I refused to continue dating a liar!

All Joe did was lie! He lied about wanting a baby and wasted precious time and money on all of the fertility treatments I took. I had so many false hopes— all because he lied! There were negative pregnancy tests, over and over again— all because of his dishonesty! Joe spoke negativity and lies about me, trying to make himself feel better, when all along, he didn't have anything going for himself in life.

At that point, I started to realize that I had been sleeping with the enemy. I used to put a fake smile on my face, while knowing deep down inside that there was nothing in my life with Joe to smile about. I was so upset that it scared me. I was stuck in a revengeful place, wanting to harm him in the worst way. So, I prayed and asked God to change my heart.

After all of the craziness I went through, I felt sorry for him. I know that the moment I left him, he would recognize that he missed out on a phenomenal woman that he would never have again. And no matter how much he searched, there would never be anyone who could cover his back the way that I did.

Despite how he treated me, I always made sure he was taken care of. Even though he lied to others, saying that I sat around the house all day, I worked two jobs, went to school, and kept the house in order. *But what did he do?* Absolutely nothing! I guess he got the better end of the deal, telling everyone that he chose me! But I decided that I would not be used, so I had to let him go. I wished him well, tossed all of those old bones in the trash, and decided to keep it moving.

After having so many rocky relationships with men and other family members in my life, I didn't expect the relationship with my dad to be any different. Therefore, when he resurfaced in a *beautyfull* manner in my dream, I was shocked.

3

___________

# INTERNAL WOUNDS

hile walking down the path of the unimaginable, a shadow appeared. As it moved closer to me, I screamed, "Why didn't you protect me?" And for a moment, I was afraid until I recognized his facial structure. *Daddy! Could it really be him?* Although it looked like him, something still didn't make sense. Everything seemed real, but I knew it had to be a dream because my dad had just recently passed. But I embraced this opportunity to finally connect with him, as I was able to say everything I'd always wanted to say. I finally got to seek the answers I needed. And even though it was just a dream, it was very real to me. It was as if I could feel his love and hear his words so clearly.

"I love you," he stated, as he embraced me and wouldn't let me go. He continued, "...and you are still my heart." I asked, "Why didn't you protect me?" He replied, "I am so sorry. I know I should've protected you, but life got in the way of that." A frown took over my face because I didn't understand what that was supposed to mean. "Life got in the way of that? How?" I questioned him. "Well, it all started with me wanting to party, have fun, and be with multiple women, while I was still with your mother. I wasn't ready to be a father at a young age, but I thought I could handle it. I've made plenty of mistakes in my life and I pray that you can forgive me. I wasn't in your life like I should've been and I had an addiction that I couldn't break," he responded. "But I needed you," I went on to say. But before I could finish my sentence, he interrupted, "Yes, I should've protected you from the abuse you encountered and the lost love you were looking for."

After hearing those words, a warped sense of peace came over me. My dad may have not been around, but when he was, we engaged in meaningful conversations, as he was brutally honest. He told it like it was— no cut cost, whatsoever! And that's exactly where I got my candid nature from! I was a very outspoken girl, and I told it like it was. I was honest with how I felt, no matter what. So, I had to tell him exactly how I saw it.

* * *

*Dad, allow me to explain. I looked for you multiple times, waiting for you to come see me. Do you know how that made me feel? I grew up in a broken home and had to take care of siblings at a young age. I had responsibilities that I wasn't ready for, and had to figure out what love was all on my own. I had no clue how a man was supposed to treat a woman. You did not show me that! So, I went out into the world looking for what I thought was love. Misinformed! Miseducated! From what I did see, it was not love. But I learned that later on in life.*

*Dad, you were supposed to be my foundation— my foundation of love! But you withered away and left me to confide in boys that ultimately hurt me and changed my heart, forever. You missed all of my graduations. And from what I remember, you were not there! I could not attend the father-daughter dance because you were no where to be found!*

> *Intermittently, you entered in and out of my life when you*
> *wanted to. And when you did come around you, you didn't*
> *stay long because you and mom would argue, as soon as*
> *you came back around. Did you ever stop to think about*
> *how I felt? I loved you and adored being with you*
> *whenever I could. I truly cherished that little bit of time*
> *with you. But to be honest, I needed more.*

With tears falling from his eyes, he interjected, "I am so sorry." But before he could say anything else, I continued.

> *While growing up, I never heard the words, "I love you." I*
> *never heard, "I am proud of you" until after I graduated*
> *from High School. Oh, but I heard everything else though!*

> *You always told me that I was your heart. And when I*
> *managed to get a few minutes of your time, you said you*
> *loved me. But then it made me wonder. If you say I'm your*
> *heart, how can you live without me? It's impossible to live*
> *without your heart. And does saying you love me count*
> *more than showing it?*

He didn't have an answer. In fact, I could barely see him. He began to fade, as he slowly walked away. I begged him to stay, but he said he had to go. Tears fell from my eyes, as I cried for a moment, but then decided to continue along my path. Then, without warning, the dream suddenly shifted. Someone else approached.

As I was walking, a woman tapped me on my shoulder. "Well, hello there," she said. "Hi," I spoke back. I couldn't believe it! It was my sister! And to be honest, I really didn't want to sit and talk with her. Nevertheless, I decided to hear her out.

"I know I am the last person you want to speak to," she started to say. And she was absolutely right! Don't get me wrong, I love my sister, but our relationship changed drastically over the years. I learned that I had to love her from a distance— from the long end of the stick, if you know what I mean! After everything that took place, she almost destroyed me.

*Let's pause the dream and allow me to explain...*

A few years ago, she decided to steal my identity and use my name for her personal pleasure. She used my identity to buy cars, secure her tags, and for other expensive items. And as a result of her dishonesty, I had ten charges pending against my name. At the time, I just moved from West Baltimore to White Marsh. After a couple of months went by, I received mail from the court system with pending charges. I was shocked because I knew I wasn't at fault for any of it. At the time, I was a nursing student, working hard to better myself.

For the life of me, I couldn't figure out why I received those charges. So, I decided to call the number on the paper. The woman on the other end asked me some personal questions and finally said, "If you didn't do this, then who would have all of your information to put this in your name?" I literally had no clue! I tried to explain that to her, but she refused to accept my explanation. But before we got off the line, one thing came across my mind to ask her. "What type of vehicle are you referencing and what's its tag number" I asked. When she replied with the information, I immediately knew it wasn't a car I'd ever owned. But after putting two and two together, I discovered that it was my sister who'd put this vehicle in my name.

Immediately afterward, I called my sister. And believe it or not, she had some nerve to get upset when I confronted her about the situation. I did everything I could to try to resolve things peacefully with her, but she was not being agreeable. I was furious. I worked very hard to get to where I was and I didn't want anything to mess that up. So, I didn't have any other options left. I got a lawyer.

When I first contacted my lawyer, he didn't believe me at first. But once I showed him the evidence, he quickly saw the facts. I didn't want to have to go that route, as I felt bad for giving the lawyer all of the information I found out. I felt like I was being a snitch, but I realized I had to fight for my life, regardless of who I was fighting against. It was painfully obvious that my sister didn't care about me, so I had to take action on my own. Thinking that everything was being resolved, another issue surfaced. Another charge appeared in my name. This time, my sister got pulled over and used my name. I was enraged! *What!* I just couldn't catch a break! So, I went back to meet with my lawyer. He decided that it was best to go to the police station.

While walking into the police station, I was furious. They treated me as if I was guilty of a crime. My insides were screaming loudly! *Why am I here? Why would my sister do this?* But as soon as the officer saw me, he said, "This is not the woman I pulled over." Instead, he described the woman he pulled over. He described my sister to a T! After realizing that it wasn't me, I was free to go. I was released.

As time went on, I came to the conclusion that my life was turned upside down. I couldn't t concentrate. I cried every night. I was filled with so much heartache and pain. I just couldn't figure out why my sister would do that to me! *Of all people, my own sister?* I would never hurt or harm my own sister! I loved her and her children. We were family. I took care of her and my nephews, as if her sons were mine. I couldn't imagine myself doing such a hurtful thing to her! After struggling with this for so long, I became depressed and full of hate. I realized that if my own blood sister would do that to me then everyone else in the world would eventually do the same. So, I was filled with so much anger and hatred. I started to hate everyone and my heart grew cold.

At that point, I was done with people! I'd been getting screwed over, so I didn't have a heart for anyone else. It seemed like my family went against me because I decided to get a lawyer and fight it. Everyone called me to ask if I was going to press charges against her. All they seemed to care about was the fact that she had children and that I shouldn't take the situation to court. *But what about my life? Was I supposed to do five years for a crime I didn't do and lose everything I worked so hard for?* Absolutely not! It bothered me for a bit, but later, I realized that I did nothing wrong. If it was really about the kids, then my sister would've been thinking about her sons before she did what she did!

And with so many thoughts raging through my mind, I prayed and prayed, only to come to the same conclusion that I was moving forward with my decision. I didn't want any harm done to her; I just didn't want to take the fall her actions. So, I moved forward with my decision. I had peace about what I know I needed to do.

The day finally came; we went to court. I was so nervous that I had bubble guts. I didn't want to deal with it anymore. I had built up so much hatred in my heart that my blood started boiling. Meanwhile, the case proceeded and the judge examined all of the evidence. The whole situation was laughable because the day my sister committed the crime under my name was the day I was at work. That wasn't even smart! So, after the judge explored all of the evidence, the verdict was in. She ruled in my favor and ordered her to do several hours of community service. That was fine for me, because I never wanted her to go to jail. She had children and I didn't want my sister or the kids to suffer. I just wanted to be free of the charges that were pending against me.

After the verdict, the judge asked my sister, "Would you like to apologize to your sister?" With her arms folded, she just stared at the judge. The judge asked her again and she said nothing. I wanted to break down and cry, but I couldn't allow her to see that. I put on a front, as if I had a hard shell, when really, I was as soft as cotton on the inside. *Talk about pain! Wow!* That was the worst pain I'd ever encountered. I wouldn't wish that heartache on anyone.

Then, the judge proceeded to ask me, "Would you like a restraining order?" I quickly responded, "No," because I still wanted to see my nephews and I didn't want anything to stop me from spending time with them. After my response, the court session quickly came to an end. We all left the courtroom separately, but ran into each other outside.

Standing beside each other, face-to-face outside of the courtroom, my sister's countenance was blank. Despite all that happened, she still didn't express any remorse. She looked at me, but still didn't say anything. I was so angry that I wanted to explode right then and there. I was so hurt by her lack of regret. In that moment, I was so glad that my sorority sister came with me to court. She calmed me down and kept me from going off. Based on the way I was feeling, I may have went to jail for taking out my anger on my sister. So, I knew I had to leave right away. Therefore, I quickly went to my car, where I cried like a baby for a few minutes. I never experienced pain like this before.

After the court case, the drama didn't stop. My sister continued talking bad about me to others. She told people that I was trying to get her locked up and that I was a snitch. Being in the black community, a snitch was not a label that I wanted to have. I was so enraged, but mostly heartbroken. All of this drama affected me deeply.

When I reflect back on all that took place, it brings back painful memories and tears to my eyes— especially now that my sister is currently in prison for a crime that she committed. And because of my heart for her, I regularly send her money and still help out with my nephews.

While incarcerated, she expressed remorse. She went on to say that she was sorry and that she shouldn't have done what she did. I was relieved to hear her apology, although I couldn't honestly assess if it was sincere or not. Perhaps she understood everything clearly now that she was in prison, or it could have very well been a cover-up. Either way, I didn't have time for games.

To this is current day, I am still affected by her actions. I try to trust, but I always feel like most people don't have good intentions. As a result, I went to therapy for two years to address the stunt she pulled against me. And on most days, I feel good, but on other days when I see other families— other sisters sharing their love for one another— I pray, wishing I had that type of love with mine.

Trust is hard for me. Once it is broken, it is very hard for me to trust that same person again. I tend to give people so many chances and passes, that once I've come to the end of my rope, I'm finished. And when I'm done, I'm done. That's that! So, I knew it would take a long time to repair the betrayal and hurt I felt in my heart. It wasn't something that could happen overnight. I knew it would take time. It was a process.

But for some reason, I felt bad. And I didn't know why, but the guilt ate me up! *How could I possibly feel bad when I did nothing wrong?* I was an awesome sister to her. She treated me horribly, but I was left to face the repercussion of guilt. That really bothered me— heavily!

*My dream continues...*

So here we are— face-to-face— and I was the one who didn't have anything to say! But the shocker was that she had a lot to say— an apology! *Wow!* And at that very moment, I listened carefully and tried to understand her point of view. But although her rationale didn't make much sense at all, I just accepted it, because I knew that it was not going to get any better than that! And as a matter-of-fact, I was throughly tired of playing games. I had accepted foolishness all of my life and that was a problem that eventually made me distance myself from people, in general. And although I was tired of dealing with drama and mess, I truly desired for things to be better between my sister and me. It was just too hard for me to put my guard down again. I felt like I needed to guard my heart from family. Realizing that I felt that way was horrible, but I continued to allow her the opportunity to express herself.

She explained how she missed me and the good times we had in our earlier years. I embraced her because some part of me still loved her— *she will always be my little sister*. But then, all of a sudden, she began to walk away. As she walked away, she asked me not to turn my back on her, as she would never violate our trust like that again. I promised her that I wouldn't. Then, she disappeared, and I continued along my path.

While embracing my journey ahead, I thought about all of the people that I came across in my life up to this point. I encountered some loving people, although I felt that some came into my life at the wrong time.

*A moment of reflection...*

After my abusive relationship, I met a guy who wanted to hang out and just spend time together. But I wasn't with it. So, I brushed him off with the quickness and knew he wasn't going to hang around for too long. Prior to him, I had just lost my niece and was with a guy who didn't support me at all.

Losing my niece was a horrible experience. I pretty much lost my mind. I wasn't able to properly grieve because everyone around me wanted me to be strong and be the bigger person. They wanted me to help with planning the arrangements, when all I wanted to do was cry all day and be alone in a corner. And at the time, I didn't have support from the guy I was with. He told me to let it go and to allow her to rest. *Do you know how bad I wanted to punch him?* But let me not go there!

I learned so much from this experience. Life will definitely show you the truth, no matter if you can see it or not. And a lot of things I was blinded to, probably due to the love I had for others. But after my experiences, I was at the point where I didn't care at all! While thinking aloud, I said to myself, "Do not feel that way! There are some good people in the world!" I wanted to believe my thoughts, but at the time, I just couldn't. I was in too much pain.

*My dream continues...*

Moving along my path, I came across my dad again. He asked to hold my hand. When I gave him my hand, I immediately felt *beautyfull*. It took me back to a time in Middle School where we had a father-daughter dance. I was so happy to see him in my dream. My heart was pure again and I was elated.

Looking me in my eyes, he told me how much he loved me, and that he would always be there to protect me. Next, he placed a necklace around my neck and told me to never take it off. He kissed my forehead and told me, again, that he loved me, and that I would always be his heart.

We danced, and while spinning me around, we lost each other's hand. I looked around to see where he went. But this time, I did not feel incomplete. I did not feel empty. I knew I would see him again. The smile on my face was priceless. It was stuck and could never be removed. Because of that moment with my dad, I felt whole, secure, *beautyfull*, and important again!

After tossing and turning, I woke up sweaty and in a panic, realizing that it was all a dream. *Wow— what a dream!* It felt so real and the necklace my father gave me was still on my neck. I cried tears of happiness as I reclaimed the love I lost and the confidence I gained back.

4

# MENTAL MOVEMENT

riving the down the street, I could hear the song "Because of You" by Kelly Clarkson playing low on the radio. I turned it up so loud because I loved that song. It had so much meaning and truth to it. Not to mention, I could relate to it in every way possible.

Singing out loud, "Because of you, I never stray too far from the sidewalk... because of you, I learned to play on the safe side, so I don't get hurt," I began to reminisce about my life. Suddenly, this weird feeling came over me, as the song continued to play, "My heart can't possibly break when it wasn't even whole to start with!" *Whew*! I started to cry. My body trembled, and I felt this emptiness overwhelm my soul. It felt like a big pill was sitting in my throat that I was trying to swallow. That one verse hit like a tornado. It was hard to hold back the tears that poured out like a rainstorm.

As I poured my heart out, I felt so empty inside. I felt like I never had a good start at love. And to be honest, my heart was broken ever since I was a kid. So hearing those words really made me realize the truth of the matter. That verse had so much power. It showed me that my heart hadn't been whole to start with, due to all that I encountered in my childhood. I had hatred inside of me from seeing how men treated my mom and from my dad not being consistent in my life. I was truly messed up.

Buried within myself, I had so many emotions that I knew I had to get out before I arrived at my destination. So, I just sat there and cried, praying to God.

> God, please restore my heart and make it whole. Overwhelm
> me with Your love and show me the way out of this mess.
> Allow me to accept who I am and offer love to others.

I wanted to accept love, but my heart had been ruined for quite some time. As the song continued to play, I got lost in the words. I started picturing myself singing the song and realized that the smile I wore everyday was a fake. "No!" I said to myself, "I will not fake another smile again." I deserve to be happy and that's exactly what I'm going to be. I don't care if I need to eliminate people who are holding me back, just to be happy! I'll even eliminate parts of myself if I need to! I was ready to get rid of my negative thoughts, brokenness, and baggage I accumulated along the way.

I kept praying and praying until I felt my soul regenerated. I asked God to help me through this challenging time. And as I spoke to God, the enemy challenged every word I said. It was as if the enemy was looking right at me, telling me to drive my car off the bridge, while God stood firmly, reassuring me that I could get through this. But to be completely honest, I really wanted to just end it all. But I decided that I would get up and work hard to shake this feeling.

Battling this situation wasn't new. I've encountered multiple instances where I faced God and the enemy battling for my soul at the same time. It would often manifest as thoughts stuck in my mind, despite my attempts to remove them with prayer and positive thinking. But my negative thoughts often won the battle, as most of the negativity was based upon issues I'd been dealing with my whole life. Being there for others was no problem for me, but I couldn't be there for myself in that moment. It took me a while; however, I encouraged myself to get through my brokenness and restore myself. I stopped crying, spoke greatness over myself, and made a critical choice that changed the direction of my future. I decided to go back to therapy.

Deciding to go back to therapy was hard, but it was needed. I even spoke to my family about it, which was difficult to do because in the black community, you're supposed to be strong and not need a *shrink* to help you. Having a shrink was seen as a disgrace in the black community. My family told me that I was already strong and that I didn't need therapy. They thought it didn't work and was therefore, not needed. But I'm not sure what they saw. *Me? Strong? What exactly is strength? And how am I strong?* On the exterior, I may have looked strong, but on the inside, I was extremely weak and fragile. No one could understand how broken I was on the inside. So, I continued to move forward with my decision to attend therapy, because I knew that it was the best decision for me.

I went to therapy with an open mind, hopeful that it would help me. And honestly, it did help. I was able to speak my truth without someone telling me to wipe my tears, be strong, and do what I need to do! Basically, I was able to speak my truth without being shut down. Around my family and friends, I couldn't cry because that was a sign of weakness. Some people just didn't want to hear it. But therapy helped me to get it out. There were times when we spoke and I would explode with tears because I had so many emotions that I never let go of. I forgave a lot of people, but the pain of the memories was still there. Forgiveness does not mean that I've forgotten. All of the pain was stored deeply within me. All of the negative spirits from multiple men were left inside me— literally. And this caused me to wonder. *How many times have I allowed people to leave their negative spirit around me or within me?* I carried those unhealthy spirits with me and I had to shake it off of me or find some way to remove them. So, continuing my therapy really helped me to do just that!

Over the next few months, things were great. I was in a positive state of mind. Following the directions of the therapist helped me tremendously. I took copious amounts of notes and wrote down my feelings, which helped me walk away from situations before my frustrations got the best of me. Writing really made my days better. But it didn't last this way for too long.

Although things went well for a while, the enemy approached me with evil, but in disguise. This time, he used someone close to me to hurt me. He knew that I loved my family beyond measure and that strangers didn't have the ability to negatively affect me as much. Therefore, he used a family member to harm me.

I was approached by a close family member who needed support. So, I did what I could to help because I saw that he really needed it. I allowed him to use my car. But months later, he destroyed it. He had crashed my car and left me with the bill. He didn't pay for any of the damages that he caused. And because of that, I was hurt. But it hurt even more because we were very close. After learning about the damages, I received a phone call stating that my car was in an accident and hit a person. I was extremely upset because this vehicle was still in my name and I'd been paying the insurance on it, as well.

As a single woman, I had two vehicles, so I let my cousin use one of them, because I wasn't doing anything with the second vehicle, anyways. And I definitely wasn't going to allow my ex to drive it, although he wanted to! I stood up for myself and told my ex no because he'd taken enough from me already! So being the nice person that I was, I allowed my cousin to drive my second vehicle despite my name being on it. But as a consequence of the accident and my name being associated with the vehicle, the authorities came after me! I was so frustrated because I got into another situation after wanting to help out a family member! Instantly, I had a panic attack. I tried to rush into the house before the tears fell from my eyes. My body was shaking and the blood ran through my body. My heart was pounding.

Finally, I made it to the house. I got through the door and fell to the floor, begging God to hear me. I was not going to stop until He listened. I screamed for God to hear me because I knew that I needed help! *Why me, God? Why is that every time I try to help people I suffer as a* result? I was so tired of being in situations like that. My mind was too cloudy to understand what I was supposed to do from there. So, I went for my Bible and read the Book of Psalms from the beginning and did not stop until I felt safe and secure. I knew I had to keep reading until I felt confident enough that I wouldn't do anything irrational. And for several days, I stayed in the house, not wanting to be around anyone. I was stuck in a mental state of depression, trying to mentally move myself to think positive and to see a better outcome, despite all of the challenges I'd been facing.

One spring day, I sat in my bedroom spaced out. Out of all of the days that I barricaded myself in the house, this day was different. I sat in my bedroom in despair, desperately trying to understand my purpose, my next move, and how not to be in this mind state ever again. I played music, which sometimes helped, but this day, I had so much on my heart that it did not work, as planned. I was so overwhelmed, as my mind went back to all of the hurt and pain that I encountered throughout my life. *No, not this again!* I couldn't believe it was happening— *again!* So, I began to write until I got all of the words out that I needed to say.

*July 7, 2017 [9:03 PM]*

> *Entering the room, where you are solitarily confined to the walls of another galaxy, the inside seems just a bit different. You feel like the walls are caving in on you as your heart rate increases, while trying to keep yourself focused. Trying not to allow your mind to wonder, you think of a happy memory to keep yourself calm, although conformed within the walls, but it doesn't help. Should I leave, only to return to the walls that are closing in on me? Or, should I stay to face the inevitable? The wetness from my perspiration, while pacing back and forth beyond these walls, caused antagonizing thoughts. Not knowing what will happen next had me biting my lip, as I suddenly*

*switched positions from the way that I was contained
within the walls— only to realize that I was trapped and
being pulled in.*

And for sure, I was trapped, not knowing what to do next. I was tired of loving, tired of hurting, and tired of being the strong person that I needed to be on the outside, while crumbling on the inside. I was extremely tired! Trying to make something from absolutely nothing was exhausting. Having tear drops disguised as rain drops, I felt all alone. I was by myself. I felt like I received more pain than gain! And nothing eased that feeling! I was fed up and ready to give up!

I felt like saying goodbye to everyone and goodbye to life! I experienced so many emotions within a matter of minutes. It was scary how my mind rapidly traveled through so many emotions.

Reflecting back, I realized that I'd been brokenhearted from day one. From what I experienced as a child, I didn't have a healthy understanding of life and love. My heart was shattered from the beginning, and consequently, I never had a fair start. So, I decided to let out all of those feelings by writing to my dad through my journal.

*Back to my writing...*

*You looked me in my eyes and promised to never hurt me. You
promised to always love and cherish me— to be right there
by my side! But where were you? I waited to see you and to
talk to you about my day. But you showed me how to be in
and out of love, which was more than my heart could
endure. I remembered all of the times I cried when you
didn't show up. You weren't there. Love should have
started with you.*

I felt good to let those feelings go, although I felt like I had a multiple personality disorder. Having a dissociative identity was how I identified myself. Traveling through various emotions had me feeling like something was really wrong with me.

I held back my love due to experiencing so much pain and the results of toxic people. But holding my love and heart back was the only way to prevent myself from being harmed. So, I held back my tears and emotions because no one deserved my love nor my heart. I was tired of adapting to every person's request to satisfy their need. While doing so, I lost my own self! I was everything everyone else wanted me to be— to give them purpose and to please them. *But who am I?* Again, I screamed... *who am I?* I lost the very essence of my life, my voice, and my inner being. *How do I get back to me?*

I was stuck in a trance, trying to figure out why I allowed people to dictate who and what I should be. I started to remember all of the things I changed to satisfy others. The way I laughed, smiled, and walked were all under harsh criticism. *You laugh too loudly; your smile is too big;* and *you walk like a duck—* were all things I'd grown accustomed to hearing! I was called four eyes, talked about because of my thick hair, and scolded for not looking over my siblings when I had other responsibilities to take care of. So now that I look at myself, desperately trying to fit in, I realized that all of these requirements and guidelines just didn't work for me! I felt like I should've noticed this earlier in life. But at the time, I just wanted to be accepted. *And now I do! I accept myself!* And I love myself for who I am.

*I continued to write...*

> *I once had a dream that I could be anything that I wanted to be. Those days were filled with positive vibes and nothing could get in the way of my thoughts and dreams. That is, until you came along, telling me that I wasn't good enough! "Maybe you should try it this way... no this way," is what you'd say. I agreed to whatever you said, not knowing that I had lost a little of myself in the process.*

Life went on, as I tried to make the right decisions. But just like clockwork, peer pressure came to challenge me! "Girl, do it this way" is what I'd hear. But that was their idea, not mine. I'd already lost my style and originality, which blended in to become everyone else's style. And as time continued, I realized that everyone's standards weren't the same as mine. Everything related to family, dating, love, and living were all questionable. What society viewed as attractive was different from what I saw in the mirror. As a result, I began to question my beauty. So, I made changes to myself. After while, I didn't recognize myself anymore; I became unrecognizable. I'd already faced so many challenges, and yet another one surfaced.

To this day, I still fight those demons. They've intruded my family, and then, and our dynamic has changed for the worst. I'm not sure why this happened, but I knew that something had to give! This took a turn that I never expected. Never in a million years would I have thought that my family would fall apart like this.

A dangerous battle between my cousin and his mother and grandmother occurred. This violent battle should've never taken place. An altercation took place, which led my cousin to threaten his mother and grandmother's life. He told them that he was going to kill them. And he actually tried to! By manipulating the gas tank in the house, it could've been tragic! I am so glad they smelled it and immediately called for help. But trying not to think too much about this, I just prayed.

A few weeks later, one of my brothers attacked my mother. I thought to myself, I cannot believe this is happening right now. So, I spoke aloud and begged God to come over my family and protect them, because the enemy had a tight grip on them. Not knowing where things went wrong within our family, I took a look back into our past, and examined our upbringing, trying to figure out a way to fix this. Nothing came to mind, but prayer! So, that is exactly what I did.

I mentally moved my mind from negativity to positivity, so that I wouldn't be devoured by all of the drama that had been going on within my family. With every opportunity I had, I prayed, prayed, and prayed! And with everything going on in the world, this situation really showed how black women are not even protected by their own black boys that they raised to be men. *How pathetic!* Here they are—

single black women, who sacrificed everything to do what they had to do for their children— but now, the children they raised to adulthood have turned their backs on them. I refused to have my son around this. He was not about to be another statistic of this mess. Things just have to get better.

# 5

# I'VE CONQUERED

There were so many thoughts rumbling around in my head. Sometimes, it was hard to turn them off.

*"No! You cannot make it out of the ghetto!*
*No! You are not as fortunate as others!*
*No! You will not have a fair fight!*
*But— yes— you will be a statistic!*
*Yes! It will be much harder for you!*
*Yes! You will have to work ten times harder than others!*
*Yes! Regardless of your title, people still won't respect you."*

Playing like a broken record— over and over— those were the words of everyone around me. But I was determined not to be a statistic. I was determined to prove to myself that I can have better! I can do better! I can be successful one day! I just happened to fall into the mischief of life.

I allowed myself to take the responsibility of vengeance into my own hands. I often reacted to what people said about me and fought others to prove a point. And that point was clear— I was not to be played with! People knew what to expect. And because of that, they knew my standard.

I was never the one to hang with a crowd or a gang of people. I flew solo. I had one best friend, and besides her, I didn't need many other females around me. But most importantly, I surely didn't want to be involved in the *he say/ she say* drama. But after making plans for my future, knowing precisely what I wanted, somehow I got sucked into the trivialities of life! I noticed that I was the one everyone called upon, whether for money, help, advice, transportation, or support for an altercation. I was the go-to girl, and boy did that cause my life a lot of headache and stress!

It was a hot summer day when I received a call from my sister that some girls had jumped her. Without asking for any details, I immediately asked where she was and met up with her. We decided to go to the location where the girls hung out. And everything started back up again because I was ready. "If anyone threatens or hurts my family, they will have to pay," I thought. And as a result of my thinking, we got into a fight with several girls.

When the police showed up, we were arrested and then pepper-sprayed. I was released because I met the age-requirement; however, my sister had to be picked up by our mother. When she arrived, she was very upset and frustrated, asking what happened and why I decided to approach the girls who jumped my sister. As I went on to explain, she told me that it did not matter. She made it clear that as the older sister, I should've made a better decision. However, I didn't know what decision she was talking about. What was I supposed to do? They jumped my sister. But I let her keep talking and just listened to what she had to say. But deep down inside, I felt like I did the right thing. And based on where we were from, you have to show people you weren't scared. When you live in the hood, you have to stand your ground, or else people would continue to antagonize you. And I was not going to let that happen! I vowed to always be there for my sister.

But not too long afterward, I was in another altercation because of my sister. My sister had issues with another girl. And that girl brought her older sister into the picture. So, when I heard about what happened, I immediately jumped into the situation.

I flew down the street to get to my sister's location. And without any words exchanged, I immediately swung my fist. I didn't care about who did what. I had the mindset of— *if you mess with my sister, you mess with me!* Anyone who had problems with her automatically had problems with me. It didn't matter who was against her. I was my sister's keeper! And even though the fight got pretty vicious, I didn't give up. The neighbors outside on the block had to break up the fight. I was surprised that the police weren't called. But I wasn't complaining; I was happy at the same time.

It all happened so fast. We jumped in our cars and sped off quickly. While calling my sister to see where she was, I noticed blood on my phone and hands. I was furious and didn't know how to calm myself down. I had scratches all over my arms and a deep gash on my face.

When I got to my sister's location, we quickly discussed how everything got started. But later, I found out that the initial version she shared with me was quite different from the version she shared a few months later. However, at the time, I wasn't aware of that. So, I just took her word for it and left it alone. After we discussed everything, I went home to get clean, praying no one spotted my license plates.

I went home, cleaned myself up, and saw that my scratches were not that bad. However, I was upset about the one on my face. But at the end of the day, we won the fight and destroyed those two girls. So, I was content about that and went on about my day.

Thinking back to this time period, my sister wasn't the only person who would call me for extra help in a fight. My cousins liked to call me, too. And because of them, I engaged in multiple fights whenever they told me someone bothered them.

Fighting was literally my life. I had so much pinned up rage and adopted the "I don't care" attitude as my motto. However, that got me nowhere, as I learned that valuable lesson later on in life. However, at the time, I didn't see it as wrong to think that way. People treated me wrong, so I felt like I had the right to treat others the same way. But things quickly changed for me after the next altercation I experienced. That fight took me out for a few days— which were more like months.

It was a winter night. However, it was a lovely day to go outside in a dress and paint the town! My sister, friends, and I decided to go to a bar lounge and have some fun. It was a great night, until the evening took a sudden turn. We were having the time of our lives— partying, dancing, and drinking! We were enjoying life!

After having a lot to drink, I needed to use the restroom. I don't usually use public restrooms, but in this instance, it was an emergency. So, I went. Soon afterward, I heard a lot of commotion. After I quickly washed my hands, I left the restroom and entered into the lounge.

When I arrived in the lounge, I witnessed my sister and friends fighting a group of girls! So, I did what I naturally do best. And because I look out for those I love, I immediately jumped into the fight. I pulled, hit, and dragged every girl that was in our way. But once security saw what was going on, they put all of us out.

While walking to my car, I noticed that the lounge was closing and letting everyone out. So, everyone decided to jump in my car, sit in the parking lot, and finish the bottle of alcohol we started drinking earlier. We continued to drink, as cars pulled out of the parking lot.

As my friend talked to a guy, I noticed a dark-colored car pull up on the driver's side of my car. At the same time, my sister was arguing with a passenger in the other vehicle. But because there were so many people in the car, I couldn't tell who she was arguing with. However, moments later, that's when things got out of hand.

My sister was so upset that she threw a wine glass at the car beside us. And immediately afterward, a fight broke out. Multiple people jumped out of the car and approached my vehicle. So, I jumped out of my car, and the battle was on!

I was stuck between two cars when a random guy approached me, trying to pull me off the girl I was fighting. I thought he was trying to break up the fight until he hit me in my face. And this irritated me even more! He repeatedly hit me, until I fell back into the vehicle. I continuously kicked him, so that he would not get to me. One of my friends noticed this and handed me a box cutter. And since the guy was so determined that he wanted my blood, I knew what I needed to do. I needed to end that battle quickly.

So, when the guy swung at me again, I decided to stab him with the box cutter. I must've stabbed him pretty severely because blood quickly poured from his body. It ran through his white t-shirt like water from a faucet. And immediately afterward, I tossed the box cutter.

On the other side of the car, the fight continued, until the crowd saw the guy that I stabbed staggering through the parking lot. I tried to leave as fast as possible, but it was too crowded, and a security officer grabbed me. I managed to slip away from him, but another security officer scooped me right up. It happened so fast that it seemed like he grabbed me with one hand! But after that, everything else went downhill.

I was in the custody of both security officers. There was no way I could've escaped either of them. So, they took me to the back lounge, where I saw my sister sitting in the hallway entrance. We were both handcuffed until the police came to take us to the precinct.

At the precinct, the police questioned and took pictures of us both. My face was severely bruised, and it was evident that I suffered significant damage. Regardless of such, I decided not to say anything about it. And despite the officers seeing how badly I was beaten, they kept threatening me about my impending consequences if the guy I stabbed didn't live.

The next morning, they hauled us off to jail. Later, I found out that I was being charged with attempted murder. I was extremely shocked to hear that! I was the victim of physical assault, yet I received a charge for a crime I committed in self-defense.

After being beaten several times by guys in my past, I was determined not to allow another man to harm me again. So, deep down inside, I truly felt as if he got what he deserved. Although I didn't want him to die, I wanted him to think twice before he ever swung at another woman again. He was truly a coward for what he did. However, he probably didn't expect what he received in return!

When I was offered a phone call, I immediately called home to speak to my mother. On the phone, I had to break the news about my charges. I couldn't help but think about what my mom previously told me about making better choices. But the more I thought about everything that took place, I realized that only my sister and I were locked up. *Where were all of my so-called friends? And where was my car?* Later, I found out that one of my friends had my things and that my vehicle was safe.

Time was not on my side. My sister was released a couple of days after our arrest, but I had to endure fifty-seven days in a nasty jail cell! I really got an opportunity to see the trashy system for what it was. The hardest part was replaying the memories over and over in my head. *Where were my friends? Why didn't I see them fighting with my sister and me? Why did my friend hand me the box cutter?* With all of these overwhelming questions and thoughts, I was beyond stressed. I couldn't believe all of this happened!

To make matters worse, I had to fight off women who were coming at me. Back then, I had long dreadlocks and a body to kill for. So, every day, I would hear the same woman trying to make moves on me. She used to call me *Dreadz*, and I hated it. So, I approached her and told her to never call me that again! Apparently, she thought I was joking. The following day, she completely disregarded what I said and commented on how thick I looked in my red suit! I was so angry that I almost went off on her. I was extremely irritated by her approach, but more frustrated that I was in a red suit.

Red suits were for people in maximum security for crimes like attempted murder and robberies. I was not a criminal! I had to defend myself against a violent man the best way I knew how, or else he could've killed me! So once again, I had to fight for my life.

I was on the verge of winning, when I defeated my offender, but in the end, the system let me down. And I was stuck. I didn't know what else to do. I went to a bail review, only to be denied and labeled as a flight risk. I was completely taken back by that assumption! I was not a flight risk. *Where in the world would I go?*

Sitting in that cell, I realized that my life was ending. It felt like I was going to lose everything— my job, my home, and my car. A few of my friends came by and put money on my commissary. I truly cared for my friends, but I knew that I had to get to the bottom of what happened. And no matter how I felt, I was prepared to accept the truth.

So, I asked them where they were, and I told them exactly how I felt. I told my friends how upset I was that only my sister and I got arrested! But in their defense, they made it appear as if they were fighting, too. They wanted me to think that the only reason we got charged was because my sister and I used weapons. But they were right, so I accepted their rationale.

My sister threw a wine glass, and I stabbed someone— but it was all done in self-defense! Everything we did was to protect ourselves! *What man jumps into a girl fight and hits another woman multiple times in the face?* Maybe he was mad that I was winning the fight. I have no idea what he was thinking! Breaking up the fight and going about his business would've been the best move for him to make. But since he wouldn't stop attacking me, I had to take action. And unfortunately, he will have a constant reminder of the bad deci- sion he made when he sees the scar on his abdomen for the rest of his life. But the more I thought about that night, the more enraged I became. My hatred grew even more for him and all of the other guys that hurt me in the past. The only person who seemed to care for me was the man who I was currently dating at the time.

When Jackson found out that I got arrested, he was furious. He kept saying, "You have so much good in your life; why did you let this happen?" But after explaining my side of the story, he understood. He felt that there should've been a consequence for the man who attacked me, but also thought that I shouldn't have been in that predicament in the first place! So, he found me a lawyer and decided to help me out.

Emotions were high, and I knew that my family was disappointed in me. *But what was I going to do?* Getting a call that I was locked up was a lot better than getting a call that I was dead. I was only locked up because I defended myself. I wasn't going to allow a man to harm me! Never again would I allow it! And I didn't care who understood my decision. That was that! In the end, I found out that the guy survived. I was genuinely happy that he lived, but I was angry that I had to be in jail for an action I committed in self-defense.

After I got over the hurdle of accepting that this problem wasn't going to change, I realized that I had to think rationally to win the battle. I knew I was intelligent, and I told myself that I could over-come this and get on with my life. I just had to think positively.

Days went by, and it felt like forever. I hated being there. People told me when to wake up and when to go to my small cell. While I was there, I met a couple of wise women who were fighting for their lives, as well. Although still incarcerated, spending time with those women made it a lot better, along with visits from my friends.

I looked forward to the visits I received from my friends because I could find out how things were going outside of jail— or so I thought! Later on, I found out everything that really took place. I discovered that they didn't tell me everything. In addition to their dishonesty, it seemed like no one cared. None of my family members visited me. I guess they didn't have time to see me. But my boyfriend regularly came by to see me.

After visits with Jackson, I would have vivid imaginations of our time together. I would go back to my cell and reminisce on all of our intimate experiences. He was about ten years older than me, but I didn't care. He exposed me to things that I never experienced before. But since I was incarcerated, all I had were memories. So, I reflected on the things we did, trying to bring them into my present.

One day, I was caught in my vivid thoughts when a correctional officer called my name. "Dixon!" she said. Immediately, my thoughts ceased. She interrupted my happiness to pick up some mail. I was not happy about the interruption, but I went to get the mail, anyway. When I got there, I realized it was from my family. However, I wasn't interested in reading it because I felt like they should've come to see me. Nonetheless, I read their mail.

When I read the letters, I received a bunch of "miss you" and "can't wait to see you" letters. *Lies*! I didn't believe anything they said. And I realized that my vivid memories were ruined because of their lies! But life had to move on, and I couldn't get those images back. So, I just went to play cards with my cellmate.

While playing cards, a familiar face approached. I couldn't believe it! The same disrespectful woman who made sexual comments about my body decided to play cards with me. She walked over to where I was and sat next to me, running her fingers through my hair. I immediately got up and threatened to stab her if she ever touched me again. And because I was keeping score in the game, I had a pen top that I could use as my weapon. I was sick and tired of her disrespect. That was her first and last warning! But because one of the correctional officers overheard me threatening her, she took me to solitary confinement and put me on psych watch! They said I was a danger to myself and others! *I couldn't believe that lie!* Nothing was wrong with me! I was just standing up for myself and wasn't going to be bullied.

After a couple of days, I was back on the tier and witnessed a church session. So, I went over and decided to join. I was so heavy and burdened. I desperately needed God to come into my life and change my outcome! I begged Him to change my thinking and my behavior. I truly wanted a change of heart!

After attending the first session, I continued to take part in the church services regularly. I attended faithfully and enjoyed every moment of being with the ladies. And for additional support, I participated in an anger management class. It helped me to realize all of the incomplete stages of my life and where my problems originated. I learned a lot about myself from attending anger management classes and church services. Both sessions helped me become the better person that I desired to be. And while I was faithful to my growth, I continued to pray throughout the process.

Life behind bars was rough, and I needed God to help me get out. I slept on the top bunk and often heard the pain of men and women being raped by fake dildos that were created behind bars. One night, I will never forget. I heard a man screaming at the top of his lungs, while his body thumped loudly against the wall. It sounded as if his mouth was held shut, while he screamed in agony. Hearing all of this pain disgusted me. There were many nights where I couldn't sleep. So, I just cried and prayed. I wouldn't wish this devastation on any of my enemies. I was desperate to get out of this pace, but I needed a way out. And finally, that day came!

After being indicted and previously denied the option of bail, the courts *finally* granted me bail. The judge saw my background and felt that I was doing good with my life. He noticed that the man who hit me multiple times had a domestic background and several charges for putting his hands on women. When I heard about his history, I felt justified about what I did. I felt that he got what he deserved. But more importantly, I was ecstatic that I had the opportunity to go home! We just had to figure out a way to pay it.

After multiple bail bonds denied me bail, one company decided to give me a fighting chance. When I called home to get an update from my lawyer, I found out that she found somebody who could help me! I was so happy that I wanted to cry. But, I didn't want to cry in front of the other women that were standing around. So, I went to my cell and let it all out. When my cellmate asked me if I was okay, I explained what happened, and she told me how happy she was for me. I was over-the-top relieved that my lawyer found someone to put up $100,000 for my bail. I didn't care about anything else— not my belongings or my food. I gave it all away to my cellmate and left my cell immediately.

While waiting for my friends to pick me up, I wanted to cry so badly, but I waited until they pulled up. They had a bottle waiting for me when they arrived, but I wasn't interested in drinking. I was too happy to be free! After fifty-seven days, I wondered how people could manage being incarcerated for several years. My time behind bars was horrific, and I never wanted to go back! Although I met some nice women, attended church sessions, and joined an anger management class, I was happy to be out.

When I arrived home, I threw away my clothes and took a shower. I put on some fresh new clothes and was determined to do life differently. But despite my plans for a better life, more pain came knocking at my door.

I learned that my friend's mother was bedridden in hospice, but wanted to leave so she could transition in her home. This weighed heavily on my heart! I refused to accept that this was happening! But despite my hurt, I went to go see her. This was not how I envisioned my first day of freedom! But regardless, I was happy to see her. We talked for a while, and she wanted me to make her a promise. She desired for me to look over her youngest daughter. And I happily agreed to do so. I had every intention of fulfilling my promise, until things changed, and we stopped communicating over a broken promise. So, I just continued to stay to myself and enjoy my newfound freedom!

Life was so good being at home instead of behind bars. I truly enjoyed every moment of it that I could. One day, I was so happy that I got drunk and apparently rolled down a hill. I don't remember anything about that incident, but I was informed about what took place. My happiness was hard to explain; I was just beyond ecstatic to be back in society! But my days of pain weren't over yet. It seemed like things from the past were catching up to me.

A couple of days later, I went to a beauty supply store on the east side of Baltimore with my friends. I planned to cut my dreads off and wanted to get hair supplies from the store. While I was in the store, I heard a loud thump. It sounded like a window was busted. When my friends and I went outside, I quickly noticed that someone threw a long two-by-four into the back window of my car. I was beyond heated! *Who in the world would do that?* I'd only been gone for fifty-seven days, and I didn't have issues with anyone that I knew of! And based on what happened, it looked as if my car was intentionally targeted! Later on, I discovered the truth. It was a lot for me to wrap my head around.

After the incident, I asked my friends what happened, and if they had issues with anybody while I was gone. Everyone said no. But because I didn't believe them, I did my own digging, only to find out the truth. What I discovered was that one of my friends drove my car around as if it was hers! Not to mention, she was messing with another woman's man! That's when I realized why my vehicle got damaged. I assumed that the woman was targeting my car, out of revenge, thinking that it was my friend's car. Once I got to the bottom of the truth, I made sure my car got fixed by those who were responsible for what happened. I refused to pay for this damage!

About a week later, my heart was devastated. My friend's mother transitioned. I was so hurt and distraught. I grew up around her for many years. Her daughters were more than just my friends; they were like my own sisters. So, to honor her life, we all went out to get tattoos of her name. It was a troubling time for all of us, but we got through it the best way we all knew how.

After while, the party life continued. But this time, I was a lot more conscious of my surroundings. I told myself that I was not getting into any more trouble. I wanted to do things differently. And thankfully, I was able to get my job back.

Later in the year, I applied to attend college and started taking prerequisite courses for nursing school. I absolutely loved what I was learning and knew that I was in the right field!

One day after class, I went to see my brother. While I was upstairs, I heard loud arguing outside, in front of his house. So, I went to see what was going on. Another one of my brothers was outside fighting! But after the fight, the person he fought decided to bring others into it. More drama! I couldn't believe this was happening. I was trying to stay away from fights and anything that could get me locked up again! It felt like I could never catch a break. So, I went outside and told my nephews to go in the house.

The drama started back up; fights broke out left and right! Everyone in the street was fighting! One girl swung at my sister; another girl swung at me. Moments later, I noticed a guy lean into his car to get something. And because I didn't know what he was getting, I quickly tased him before he could pull it out of the vehicle. He immediately fell to the ground! Soon afterward, the fight ended. His friends picked him up off the ground and carried him away.

My immediate response was to run back into the house and get rid of the taser. My irrational thinking crept back in. But in all honesty, I had to think quickly. I didn't know what he was grabbing. We all could've died. So because I was unsure of what he had, I felt like I needed to take quick action, since I was the one who saw him reach into his car for something. I couldn't afford to take any chances!

Soon afterward, the police were called. Everyone started pointing fingers at me. And back to jail I went.

Right to central booking— the last place I wanted to be! They booked my sister's ex-boyfriend and me. *Why him?* I had no idea why he was even here because he had nothing to do with the fight. But thankfully, I was let out on my own reconnaissance. I was so happy that I peed in my pants.

After being released from central booking, I knew things had to change— *for real this time*! After I caught a hack to my brother's house from central booking, I picked up my car and went home. And again, I vowed to never get into any more trouble! But somehow, trouble kept finding me!

It felt like the devil had a hold on my life! He tried to drag me down, but I wasn't going down without a fight. Daily, I fought for my life. But this time, I planned to fight in court, by simply telling the truth.

When I arrived in court, I explained what happened. I told the judge that I saw a man reaching in his car, but didn't know what he was getting. I expressed that I only tased him in an attempt to protect our lives. I truly believed that he could have killed us and that I wouldn't be alive to tell the story! But regardless of my self-defense plea, I was informed that Maryland doesn't have a "stand your ground" or "self-defense" law. I was enraged! *So, people have a right to harm me, but I don't have a right to do anything about it?* Although that infuriated me, I was just happy to be home. Therefore, I stayed far away from people and far away from trouble!

My new routine consisted of traveling to class, work, and home. I made it my business to go straight home after work. I was not visiting anyone or getting entangled with others' mess! If anyone wanted to see me, I told them to come to my house. Other than that, I wanted no parts of hanging out or going to see anyone. It seemed like everywhere I went, I had a target on my back. But no matter what, I stayed focused on my classes.

I enjoyed attending class and interacting with my classmates. We had thought-provoking discussions in class. However, there was one conversation that really stuck out to me. I had an in-class discussion with a classmate about two issues that she stood firmly in support of.

She believed that previously incarcerated individuals were more likely to get locked back up and that a person who grows up in the ghetto is more likely to stay in the ghetto. And, although I listened to her views, I made sure to share my thoughts on both matters! I agreed that it can be challenging to escape the ghetto, but that it can definitely happen! I also informed her that the assumption shouldn't be made that leaving the ghetto can't be done. I also expressed that once a person is locked up, it doesn't automatically mean that they will re-offend a subsequent time. After experiencing my own challenges, I was determined to make sure that I never got locked up again! But even though I did, I wasn't in custody for long. And after that second experience, I was even more determined to avoid all potential drama that could result in getting arrested. Therefore, I was adamant about expressing my side of the conversation with boldness and truth.

While speaking with my classmate, my emotions started to rise. I had a firsthand experience with our discussion topic, so my passion began to seep through. The conversation naturally grew into a manageable, yet heated debate. But at the end of the day, I realized that it was best to just listen to her opinion and accept it for what it was. I knew my truth, and that's all that mattered. I didn't have to prove anything to her or anyone for that matter. I had a life to live, and although I was still trying to find my purpose, I knew that it didn't involve incarceration!

Many years passed, and I finished my prerequisites for nursing school. I started my nursing classes in the fall of 2010. I was excited to do something new that would bring much success for me in the future! However, the pain of passing my classes weighed heavily on my heart. I was in a relationship with Chris, and it was hard to focus on schoolwork while being with him. Life with Chris was a disaster.

I had many fights with my boyfriend Chris, which negatively affected my ability to focus. Oftentimes, I had to remind him to tell his son to lower the noise, so that I could focus on studying. He took me for granted and didn't respect my wishes in my own house. He didn't have an education or a job, so it was hard for him to understand the importance of me trying to focus on school to get ahead in life.

While being in this relationship, I learned a lot about time management and having a sound support system. Due to all of the distractions, I ended up failing a course and started to feel down. It really hurt watching most of my classmates graduate with an AA in Nursing, while I stayed back trying to play catch up. As a result, I became discouraged, and was no longer happy with how things were going for me in school or my relationship. It felt like I just couldn't pass my classes, and that no one understood me or cared about how much completing school meant for me. But no matter what, I continued to push.

Finally, I graduated with an AA degree in psychology and continued my journey to a university afterward. My next task was to pass the entrance tests to get in! That required lots of studying, which was hard to do at home. My ex-boyfriend was a major distraction, but I continued to fight to achieve my goals! And I did!

When I heard the news, I was ecstatic! I was accepted into the nursing program! This gave me so much joy, but also major difficulty! The courses were extremely hard, and I couldn't study at home because it was not a suitable place to focus. I had to go to study halls and even other friends' homes to study. I couldn't believe that I had to do this! I should be able to study in my own home. There was too much drama going on with Chris. But I knew that it would have to end soon.

One day, Chris called me and asked when I would be coming

home. I gave him a time, but because my study session started earlier, it allowed me to finish sooner and come home earlier.

When I got home, I discovered that his son's mother had been in my house. I was livid and ready to explode! He knew she had a problem with me and started drama between us through communicating lies to his other child. But because I remembered the vow I made to myself, I was determined not to do anything that would get me locked up! I was so angry about how sneaky he was, but even more furious about the fact that he lied to me. So, I packed my things and left. That was the only way I knew how to prevent myself from getting locked back up!

Despite his wishes, I left. Chris begged me to come back home, but I didn't budge. But after a few days, I did. I wanted to make things work, but I wasn't going to be his fool. My gut feeling was that Chris wanted to know what time I was coming home to have his ex-girlfriend out of the house in time. So, then my mind wandered. *What were they really doing in there?* And even if he told me it was nothing, I still couldn't believe him. After all, he lied about her being there in the first place!

And even though it wasn't the best decision, I continued the relationship with Chris, feeling miserable on the inside. I faithfully wore a fake smile, while making plans to leave, as soon as I finished school. But there was a monkey wrench thrown into my plans! I didn't anticipate his son's mother starting more drama.

I never understood why she wanted to bother me. I did everything I could to help her son succeed. It seemed to me that she was still interested in Chris. Apparently, they still had a thing going on! Chris constantly defended and took up for her. It was easy to see that something was going on between them behind the scenes!

And as a result of dealing with so much drama at home, I often went to class upset and unable to focus. Chris and I argued many nights. And as a result, I stayed awake many nights, contemplating how to get back at him! I was so angry that I wanted to really hurt him! We had so many arguments, that it was hard to keep track of the issues we were dealing with. And many times, I discovered that he not only lied to my face, but also talked about me behind my back!

On top of that, his son's mother started to become disrespectful toward me. So, I found myself sitting outside of her house, waiting to confront her. I was tired of her mouth and wanted to do something about it! But she left her house before I arrived. And at that moment, I knew something was going on! So I went home, and was ready to put an end to all of the nonsense.

During our argument, I blacked out. I could only remember bits and pieces of what happened. I remembered pulling out the knife and cutting Chris' wrist after he punched me in the stomach. Everything went haywire! That entire night was a disaster, and I had to calm myself down so that I wouldn't go back to jail for the rest of my life.

After that day, nothing was the same. He started to say things that got under my skin. I was even more enraged when he referenced my niece's death, as if it meant nothing! I couldn't believe he had the nerve to comment on her passing! At in moment, I knew it was time for me to leave the house, right away!

While driving on the highway, I knew I had to get far away from him. So, I decided to leave. He was going nowhere in life, and I didn't want to be apart of that disaster.

But despite the facts, it was hard to let go. I was an emotional wreck. I loved Chris too deeply. I changed who I was and made financial decisions that were in his best interest. I moved from where I previously lived to Pennsylvania Avenue and MLK Blvd, so that Chris could be close to his son. But he really just wanted to be down the street from his son's mother!

It didn't take long for me to realize that every decision I made in the relationship was for him, not for us. I failed to consider my own interests, and I was headed down a path that was destroying me! I was so overwhelmed with Chris' drama that I couldn't focus on school.

One night, I dreamt that the devil was pulling me to hell. And in the dream, I woke up with Chris holding my hand. Immediately, I knew I was sleeping with my enemy and I had to move on quickly.

But it was hard to accept what I needed to do because I loved him so much.

Because of my feelings for Chris, I was up late crying one night. I was hurt and in pain after realizing that I loved Chris more than I should've. I realized that he didn't deserve me. I knew it would hurt to let go, but I knew that I had to! There was no security in the relationship and I was not safe. Chris did not have my back! And that hurt me so deeply. So, I put on my music, jumped in the shower, and cried my eyes out.

My shower was my safe place, and I knew that I could cry without anyone knowing what was going on. I needed to let out that one last cry before putting my boots on for war! I had to face the reality that it was time to leave— for good. It was tough, but I realized that I had to fight for myself.

The very next day, I had an exam, but I couldn't focus. It was extremely hard to concentrate after what took place the night before. But surprisingly, I passed! I was really happy about that. However, I still don't know how I passed because I could barely focus. But regardless, I passed!

Soon afterward, I found a place and left. Chris must have thought I was joking because he asked me to come over to watch a movie the same day I left. I declined. My focus was on myself and finishing school. I was no longer interested in entertaining a man who didn't do what it took to keep me. So, I made my boundaries clear and moved on with my life.

As soon as that chapter of my life was over, I was sure that things would get better. But semester after semester, it became increasingly harder to maintain my grades! I failed one class, and the professor had the nerve to look me in my face and tell me to consider dropping nursing school. I wanted to punch her in the face for what she said. I was angry. I couldn't believe that instead of empowering me, I was degraded by another black professional woman telling me I should drop nursing school and consider another career.

But despite her painful words, I steadied the course. I decided not to drop nursing school. And although it took me longer than others, I finished. It was one of the most painful academic experiences I'd ever faced, but I made it.

In school, I experienced mixed emotions and didn't always have the same type of professional support. Some of the professors did not care, but a lot of them did. One, in particular, spoke life over me and prayed with me. Little did she know, my dad had recently passed during my first semester at the university, and I was prepared to drop a class, until we talked and she prayed for me. And because of that day, I decided to keep pressing forward.

I realized that I could make it in nursing school, despite all of the pain and hurt I endured. My strength came from knowing that my dad would have been proud of me for finshing school; he wouldn't have wanted me to give up!

Many days, I cried and even considered starting over at another university, but I didn't. I was determined to dispel the status quo and turn every disappointment into a victory! I put in a lot of work, so I looked forward to the day where I could finally say that I conquered! I won! Having that goal as my driving force was monumental. I used it as a mechanism to keep me pushing throughout school. I couldn't believe it, but things were finally coming together. I made it to my last year of nursing school. And even more surprising, I was in a better relationship with a guy that cared for me. But there was another surprise! I found out that I was pregnant.

When I discovered that I was pregnant, my first thought was of confusion. *Why is this happening during my last year of nursing school?* I finally made it to my last year after experiencing so much pain in my previous years. But then I realized, being pregnant was my blessing. I had been trying for many years, and doctors told me that I wouldn't be able to have children. But I truly believe God turned it all around, showing me that I could have a child and be a mother.

Exactly three weeks before my last semester started, I gave birth to my son. After my son was born, I was determined to continue and finish school. But another surprise occurred!

Toward the middle of the school year, COVID-19 broke out! It seemed like the enemy was back to his same schemes. But I wasn't moved; I knew I had a lot to accomplish. And I did.

And although I didn't get to walk across the stage and receive the acknowledgment that I longed for, I was able to complete two majors. And that was enough for me! I earned two baccalaureate degrees—one in nursing and the other in psychology! I was the very first person in my family to accomplish this. I turned every setback into an opportunity to defy the status quo and establish my own legacy. I made it through that fight, and I will continue to prevail.

# 6

## CLEAR THE ATTIC

*C*onquering my academic goals was a huge step in the right direction, but I knew I was far from finished. Having this victory just launched me further toward the next— me! I needed to repair myself. But first, I had to clear the attic!

All of the toxic clutter inside my heart and mind needed to be removed and permanently destroyed. *But where do I start? How do I clear out years of pain and turmoil?* I had to take my life back, piece by piece, but I had to do it with peace within myself. No more negativity! All positivity! I decided that I needed a healthy new start! I needed a new way of thinking.

I was beyond happy to get started with my next task because I knew this would be monumental for me. Therefore, I didn't want to rush. I took my time with my progress. So, I hit the floor, crawling.

Up until then, I didn't feel that I had purpose in life. My life consisted of desperate prayers, daily requests to make it from one second to the next. I went to church and got baptized, but I still felt stuck. It felt good to take that step, but I wondered why my life wasn't progressing. A voice in my head said, "Change your surroundings," so I did. I finally understood what I needed to do. I had to change my company and the people I associated with to fulfill the life God planned for me.

In order to change my environment, I had to make crucial decisions. And to do this, I knew I needed to continue therapy and address some of the deep-rooted issues that I faced regarding trusting others. I also started going back to church and began reading the Bible. Having a strong mental and spiritual foundation really helped me along the way.

As part of my change process, I reached out to those I offended and apologized for my unhealthy behaviors. And even though many of those individuals didn't apologize for their role in the situation, I understood that my apology was for me, not others!

Over time, I built up so much anguish and hatred toward those who brought pain into my life. But I wanted it to be gone. So, I did an internal assessment and decided to release those burdens from my past— piece by piece. I needed to start with my dad, but I had to take a different approach because he was deceased. *So, I decided to write...*

* * *

*Dad, I pray your journey to heaven was wonderful. I am glad that you didn't have to suffer anymore.*

*The last time I saw you, I rushed to the hospital after getting a call that you transitioned. I ran to the room where you were and saw dried tears on your face and felt that your body was warm*

*In an instant, so many thoughts ran through my head. I tried to figure out what your last thoughts were and why you were crying. Did you know you would pass away? Did you have something you wanted to say to your children before your final breath? I wondered for a while, but regardless of what it was, I would've loved to hear your voice one last time.*

> *Dad, I love and forgive you for the times you were not in my*
> *life when I really needed you to be. I don't want to hold on*
> *to the pain from when I was a little girl— waiting for you*
> *to pick me up or your phone call. I held onto all of that*
> *pain from my childhood and grew up with hatred in my*
> *heart.*

> *All I wanted was you. I wanted your love and your attention.*
> *But because I couldn't have it, I went out into the world to*
> *fulfill that void. And as a result, I allowed myself to receive*
> *unhealthy attention from guys who abused me.*

> *Despite all of that pain, I am thankful for the times that we*
> *did get a chance to speak. You always told me to be strong*
> *and to say how I felt. You were a "no-cut-cost" type of*
> *person and was straight to the point. You were one of the*
> *most honest people I knew, and I thank you for being you!*

* * *

After releasing my heart to my father, I decided to speak with my mother face-to-face. So, I called and asked to take her out. We went to a nice restaurant, and of course, I was nervous to start up the conversation. But somehow, I worked up the nerve to say what I had to say.

> *Mom, thank you for showing me what it means to be*
> *dedicated! You've shown me how to work hard, get what I*
> *want, and end up where I want to be in life. I learned a lot*
> *from you as a child. But I struggled with having the*
> *responsibility to care for my siblings as a young child*
> *growing up, myself!*

And, of course, she tried to explain, but I just wanted her to listen. It was no one's fault.

*Listen... Mom, I forgive you! And I love you so much! You stuck it out being a single mother with six children to raise on your own. I applaud you!*

*You are an example of a bomb mother who has the strong-will and courage to do what she needs to do for her children! You didn't think of yourself. You used all of your strength for us. And because of you, I learned how to be a hardworking mother to my child, as you were with us!*

*You picked up so many responsibilities that our fathers lacked, which made me see you differently.*

*You are a SUPERWOMAN! Thank you for being a great example of a strong, productive, determined, motivated, hardworking woman. You put a new definition in the dictionary for mother! Thank you!*

* * *

Next, I called an old friend of mine. It was weird because we had an altercation over an old boyfriend, and we hadn't communicated since then.

I reached out to her on social media because she just had a baby. I wished her well and told her how beautiful her daughter was. Then, I apologized for the role that I played in the situation that caused us to stop speaking to each other. I was glad that she accepted my apology. However, she didn't feel the need to apologize for what she did. Although I was disappointed, I knew that my goal was to apologize for my wrongdoing. So, I was relieved that I had the opportunity to do that. And after I received her forgiveness, it was time to move on.

Next, I wanted to reach out to my sister. But since my sister was not around, I was unable to reach her. I tried to get in contact with her, but to no avail. So, I asked God to heal my heart of the pain I endured during our harmful interactions. And, of course, I had to express my heart through words. *So, that's exactly what I did...*

* * *

*First and foremost, let me say that I love you and want nothing but the best for you! But this drama between us is not healthy; it's not for us. As sisters, we need to have a great bond and have love for each other.*

*Now, I'm not sure where things went wrong between us or why you felt the need to harm me, but I've forgiven you for it multiple times. Unfortunately, after so many times, I got tired and frustrated. I was completely through with it! And I washed my hands of the situation because I was done.*

*But today, I want to forgive, forget, and move on. I don't want to harbor any ill-feelings or anger toward you!*

*Life for us should be different. We should be sipping mimosas, while looking at beautiful views over the hilltops. I should be showing you how to be successful. I have always admired being a role model for you. I just desire to be there for you in a healthy way.*

*So, let's move forward in love. No more disrespect! No more bitterness! Just all love, hugs, and kisses! I love you so much!*

* * *

Looking back over all of the relationships and abuse I endured, I felt bad for the guys who treated me wrong because they never got an opportunity to see me for who I really was. I just wanted love— not pain. *So, I went on to say...*

* * *

*Look at me for who I am. Do you really know me? Have you taken the time out to get to know what I like or what I love? Can you see my true self? Or, did you stay around just to get what you wanted and play games?*

*I wanted to experience pure love. I needed to have security and feel safe with the one I loved. But instead, I received black eyes, a bloody nose, bruises, a broken heart, frustration, psychological issues, and emotional weakness. I will never thank you for what you did. I just wish you could've opened your eyes to see the realness and true love I had for you.*

*I sacrificed to be with you. Did you? If you opened your eyes to see me for who I am, you would've noticed my strength. You would've recognized that I had to be strong for the both of us.*

*I only wanted the best for you. I tried introducing you to books and knowledge, but you didn't receive any of it. You were far more interested in cheating and playing psychological games. You were manipulative, but in the end, you lost a real woman.*

*I am far from angry, so please don't confuse my words. I am completely over you, which is why I left.*

*I genuinely love black men, but I have to get something off my chest. Many of you need to take a good look at who you are and what you've become. Many of you need to understand that you must take responsibility for your actions. Perhaps you didn't have a role model while growing up; maybe you didn't have anyone to show you how to love and take responsibility for your actions. Or, perhaps you don't realize that there's a problem! I understand; it's not your fault.*

*I've carried old, past hurts for some time. And many burdens have lingered within my heart. But I had to let it go. Of course, letting go doesn't happen overnight, but I had to take that step! I genuinely pray you have a good life, even though it will not be with me. And with that being said, please take care. Goodbye!*

* * *

After writing my heart out to all of my abusers, I realized that I needed to express my sympathies to the one who got away— or should I say, the one who never got the chance! We both really desired to have a relationship, but the opportunity never presented itself. But because I realized that I still had feelings for him, I wanted to express my heart to him, too.

*Mr. Pusha, you were special to me, and we genuinely liked each other. But I knew that we couldn't put actions into our feelings. We had a chemistry that couldn't be explained in words. It couldn't compare to anything I'd ever experienced before!*

*We were in a place where the walls between us were translucent. Our minds were intertwined. We thought the same thing, but didn't want to say anything out loud. We just allowed our bodies to speak for us. Energy increased! Walls secreted! Passion erupted! We locked eyes, as we danced gently, with a rough push that had me weak. My eyes closed to savor each explosion. You softly whispered in my ear. Look at me! The fire in your eyes enticed me. You were one with my body. My nonverbal cues revealed to you that I wanted more. I continued to stare at you, not losing a second of eye contact. You teased me with each push until you noticed how bad my body yearned for you. You took it easy on me, only to get me to the peak of no return. Those deeper pushes mesmerized my body. I got lost in your seductive eyes. But you brought me back with your push. Our chemistry caused tension and an explosion like no other.*

*But it was more than just our physical connection. You were a great person to talk to! Thank you for all of the conversations and for making me feel special. You are remarkable. And you will truly be missed.*

* * *

I wrote until I was relieved. I got everything out. I was truly back to myself— or so, I thought.

I met a new guy, Sam, who was down-to-earth and took care of me. I loved going out with him. And to be honest, he was the first guy that routinely picked me up in his own car and took me out. This was new for me, even though I was close to my mid-30s. What a shame that it took me this long to meet a guy like Sam! I never once had to bring my purse to pay for anything, not even when we went to the casino. And we often went, as he loved to play blackjack.

In addition to receiving money to splurge at the casino, Sam gave me money to pay my bills. I enjoyed being spoiled by him, and I needed it. I never had someone do the things he did for me. But choosing to have Sam in my life was a decision that would change my life forever. I really wanted to be with Sam because he was different from everyone else I'd ever met. I wasn't a gold digger; it just felt good to be cared for.

After dating guys that did nothing for me, I understand what it meant to be taken care of. It was never about sex; it was more about experiencing something new.

He took me out of the country multiple times, and I loved it. Everything between us was too good to be true. But one day, I found out that he hadn't told me the whole truth about his life.

*Why do people keep lying to me?* I wondered why this happened to me again! I was livid, and my mind went right back to the past. I never wanted to see him again.

But a few days later, I found out that I was pregnant, and I didn't know what to do. At first, I wasn't going to tell Sam; I was just going to get an abortion. But because I was in my mid-30s and previously had problems trying to conceive, I didn't want to pass up the opportunity of motherhood. I knew that that decision would hurt my heart for the rest of my life. I was so upset, but I had to do the right thing and let Sam know.

Although I informed him, I was internally shattered. My heart and body were drowning. I knew I had to grow up quickly and take on the responsibility of having a child.

It was not easy, which is why I initially struggled with what to do. I contemplated for months on getting an abortion, so that I wouldn't have to deal with Sam. But I realized that that wouldn't have been fair to my child. My child needed a fighting chance at life. I felt that the timing and the person who I conceived with was all wrong. But how could God's timing be wrong?

I prayed repeatedly and decided that I could do it. I was determined to be the best mother that I could be— no matter what! And although I didn't want to be around Sam, I decided that we needed to be here for our newborn baby. And that, we did.

Although it seemed like a terrible idea at the time, I couldn't allow my feelings to interrupt my child's life and influence it negatively. My child deserved the best opportunity for life.

When I found out that I was having a baby boy, I was really on board with having Sam around. From my personal experiences with dating, I learned the importance of a son needing his father.

I wanted nothing but the best for my son. So, I prepared my mind to be ready. I was ready to deal with whatever life threw our way!

# 7

# NEW MEANING OF LIFE

*L*ife has a way of maturing you, even when you don't realize it. While in nursing school, I developed character as I took on various leadership positions. I was the president of the Council of Independent Organizations at Coppin State University, treasurer of Chi Eta Phi Sorority Inc., Miss Senior of Coppin State University's Royal Court, and the news editor of the Maryland Association of Nursing Students. Having these opportunities were beneficial because they helped me become my best self.

Being the President of the Council of Independent Organizations at Coppin State University helped me communicate with others without confrontation. There were many times when I wanted to speak my mind and respond to foolishness with my fist. But I learned to control my reactions and communicate more effectively. It was definitely a learning curve, but I embraced the challenge and focused on my journey.

While being a member of Coppin State University's prominent nursing organizations (Chi Eta Phi Sorority and Maryland Association of Nursing Students), I gained access to resources and learned professionalism. Being part of these two organizations allowed me to meet many influential women and learn a lot from them, as we all could relate in some way. As we all were nursing students, we all could relate to the realities of nursing school. We were accustomed to late night studying and having no personal life. Although it was challenging, being connected to these organizations enabled me to receive many rewards and scholarships.

In addition, I was a member of two non-nursing student organizations— Psi Chi, the International Honor Society in Psychology Organization and Royal Court (Miss Senior). Being a member of both organizations enabled me to give back to the community in a significant way. I enjoyed the many community service opportunities, events for mental health awareness, and opportunities to help prospective students. Community service was my passion. And I enjoyed every minute of it. It felt great to give back to the others.

Needless to say, this time in my life was great. I was busy in school and connected to positive groups of women that furthered my success in life. I especially enjoyed taking part in community service, meeting new people, and exploring all of the resources that were offered to me while in college.

My sorority sisters came into my life when I struggled with forming a healthy bond with my own sister. Having a challenging experience with my sister hindered my ability to connect with my sorority sisters because I was stubborn and did not want to open up to trust others. But because I really wanted to have the sisterhood that I never had before, I tried hard to do what I needed to do to have a healthy bond with my sorority sisters.

Each sorority sister had her own personality and was true to who she was. I appreciated that because I hadn't experienced many real people in my lifetime, outside of my best friend.

My best friend of thirty years has stuck with me throughout the pain of my past. We are still very close, and she has always been real with me. And back in the day, we enjoyed many great times together. But despite having a close relationship with my best friend and my sorority sisters, it hurt not having one with my biological sister. And although things weren't exactly how I desired them to be, I was grateful that I joined Chi Eta Phi and had great experiences with my line sisters. It was a true blessing to connect with professional black women who desired to be nurses. Their influence helped me become a better person, which helped me become a better mom to my unborn son.

As months progressed, it was time for my baby boy's arrival. Right after my gender reveal party, it seemed as though it was time for me to give birth. I was so nervous, but I was ready! I probably watched hundreds of birth videos. I asked everyone I knew about giving birth. There were many occurrences when I thought it was time to give birth, but they all were false alarms. My doctor recommended that I get induced, but the induction didn't work.

Stefan decided to come in the middle of the night, right after everyone left the hospital. My best friend, who is also his Godmother, stayed with me the entire night, but left a couple of hours before Stefan was delivered. It seemed as if he was waiting for everyone to go so he could have time with his dad and me. I don't know if that's true, but it seemed like a reasonable theory! My mother and sorority sisters came to wait, but Stefan had other plans. He came on his terms. But that wasn't the only irony of the night!

When I walked into the hospital, I felt like I was ready to give birth. It seemed like the pain was bearable without medication. Everyone laughed at me because they knew the pain would increase! At the time, I hadn't dilated much, despite all the tactics the doctors and nurses implemented. So, I assumed my delivery would be easy since I didn't feel much pain. But I was terribly wrong! When Stefan was delivered, I remember being sedated, but awake to see his little face. He didn't cry much at all. When the nurse placed him in my arms, I trembled. I couldn't believe I was a mother and that I was responsible for caring for this *beautyfull* child.

Leaving the hospital with Stefan was another story, as transitioning home presented another set of challenges. For the most part, he was a great baby and easy to care for. However, there were days when it felt like life caved in on me, and I felt completely overwhelmed. I loved my son, but I had a bad case of postpartum depression. I had to pray every second to get through the day because it felt like my depression took over me. I never harmed him. I was just mentally deprived. A lack of sleep and having no appetite most likely contributed to me being mentally weak. But thankfully, it didn't last long. I am grateful that I was able to achieve balance shortly afterward.

Every day that went by, I admired his little expressions and smile. And when we went out, he was bombarded with many compliments. So many people thought he was a girl because of how beautiful he was!

Admiring Stefan's growth made me want to grow. And as a result, I promised him that I would be the best mom I could be.

Before he was born, I started reading to him in the womb. Since then, we've been reading ever since. And as a result, he continued to enjoy our reading sessions together.

As months went on, Stefan started to develop. He began to look a little different, as his complexion changed. He even made new gestures and began to shake his head. I couldn't believe so much happened in seven months! I was blessed to savor every moment I had with him.

My entire world revolved around Stefan, and I loved it. He had my whole heart. It was true love at its finest. Loving him was the best love I could've ever asked for. I took pictures and videos of him every day. And whenever I missed him, I would watch his videos over and over again. *What a feeling, right?!*

Being with Stefan was incredible. I loved when he stared into my eyes, held my face with his little hands, or shook his head 'no' to me. Everything he did was so adorable! Experiencing love like this was truly a gift. He was my new beginning, my blessing, and my heart. His life gave me purpose.

When Stefan turned nine months old, I could feel his love for me more than ever! The glare in his eyes, as he looked at me, was the look of pure affection. And with a smile as wide as the ocean, I finally knew the real meaning of true love.

Having this love in my life was beyond what I could've ever imagined. So, I didn't want to miss a single moment of it. I paid attention to his development and encouraged his love of creativity and fun! I wouldn't trade anything in the world for the times we sang and danced together. Everything was perfect. And it all made sense. Stefan was the answer to my prayer.

I had to go through everything I experienced in order to understand my purpose. Having Stefan in my life brought true purpose and meaning. And I understood why I had to wait for a blessing like him. Therefore, showing him the meaning of true love was my mission, as I tried to express it in words.

*Stefan, this is to you...*

*Son, you are my life.*
*Your very presence gives me purpose.*
*As your mother, I will show you the beauty of life.*
*And although life is priceless, it does not cost you a thing. All*
    *of my heart is yours!*
*I love, love, love you Stefan!*

* * *

Now that I've awakened to the new meaning of life, I view life differently. I have nothing but love in my heart, and no matter what, no one will ever change that. I have a reason to live— a reason to fight. Stefan deserves it. And it's my job to nurture, love, and protect him.

I can finally relate to how parents feel when it comes to being in love with their kids. I never experienced a love like this before, and I am so grateful to have it. And as a result, I am quick to notice when I am wrong and when I need to change. Determined to succeed, I enjoy life and wait to see what the future holds for my son and me.

I am ready to acclimate. I am prepared to embrace change. Nothing in life is perfect, so I expect some days to be challenging. But with so much love surrounding me, I know that I can overcome any obstacle in my way.

I am willing and ready to be the best person that I can be! I will continue to learn, ask questions, and stay connected to positive support systems to foster positive growth. I will continue my writing journey, as much of my growth has developed from this healthy routine.

Throughout my life, writing has been a significant part of my release and my healing. So, despite the first chapter of my life coming to an end, my writing will continue. I plan to write more as my life continues to evolve.

Right now in my life, I'm enjoying every moment I have with my son and being a new nurse. And although that has its challenges, too, I look forward to sharing that journey with you next, along with Stefan.

*But until next time.....*

# ACKNOWLEDGMENTS

The completion of this book would not be possible without the faithfulness of God. He has blessed me to overcome every obstacle and strengthened me throughout every experience, ultimately shaping me into the woman I am today.

* * *

Thank you, Mom, for being that strong woman in my life. You are my first example of hard work. I love you!

Thank you, Dad, for telling me to always express how I feel. May you rest in peace! I pray that I made you proud.

Thank you, brothers and sisters, for allowing me to be of assistance when I could be! And I pray that I have been a great role model to each of you.

Thank you, Grandma, for being so much fun. I loved doing your hair and enjoyed our talks. I pray that I did well.

And to the rest of the family, thank you!

A special thank you, best friend, for being in my life since we were three years old! You always encouraged me and kept it real!

Thank you, Flatline— *even though only a few people would know this—* but, as my sorority sisters, you've helped me through a lot, especially when life for me was challenging. Through it all, you've stuck with me. And I thank every one of you. I love you all!

Thank you, Stefan, for choosing me and for allowing me to be your mother. I love you so much, Stefan. I pray that I can be the best mother for you.

And last but not least, thank you, Nicole, for being my inspiration and letting me know that I can get this done, while being a mother and a new nurse. You held my hand throughout this process, and I thank you so much.

# ABOUT THE AUTHOR

LaShanta Dixon, a native of Baltimore, Maryland, is a leader, community advocate, and nurse. But most importantly, she is a mom to her *beautyfull* son, Stefan. She holds a special place in her family, as the first of many generations to attend college. Pursuing a double major in nursing and psychology, she has a strong drive for success and achievement.

Being in the healthcare field for over 15 years, Dixon understands what it takes to serve others and give selflessly. Within her field, she's learned various strategies to collaborate with other professionals to obtain the ultimate success for every patient in her care.

Upon receiving a Bachelors degree in nursing and psychology, Dixon realized that she needed to go further. Therefore, she plans to obtain a Masters Degree to pursue a career as a Psychiatric Mental Health Nurse Practitioner

In every aspect of her life, she is led by her passion for helping others and educating communities about health maintenance and health promotion. She desires to utilize her academic background and experience to help communities heal, grow, and generate solutions to the generational problems they may face.

CPSIA information can be obtained
at www.ICGtesting.com
Printed in the USA
BVHW040557140421
R12114300001B/R121143PG603571BVX00008B/3